THE SEPOY

THE SEPOY

By

EDMUND CANDLER

GYAN

Published by

Gyan Publishing House
5, Ansari Road
Daryaganj, New Delhi-110002
Phone: 011-47034999, 9811692060
E-mail: books@gyanbooks.com

Distribution Network
gyanbooks.com
India, USA, Canada, UK, Australia, France

ISBN : 978-81-212-6494-5 (PB)
First Published, 1919

2nd Impression 2022

Printed at: Gyan Press, Delhi.

THE SEPOY
Author: EDMUND CANDLER

THE SEPOY

BY

EDMUND CANDLER

1919

TO

SIR VALENTINE CHIROL

PREFACE

ALL these sketches, except "The Sikh" and "The Drabi," were written in Mesopotamia. My aim has been, without going too deeply into origins and antecedents, to give as accurate a picture as possible of the different classes of sepoy. In Mesopotamia I met all the sixteen types included in this volume, some for the first time. My acquaintance with them was at first hand. But neither sympathy nor observation can initiate the outsider into the psychology of the Indian soldier; or at least he cannot be certain of his ground. One must be a regimental officer to understand the sepoy, and then as a rule one only knows the particular type one commands.

Therefore, to avoid mistakes and misconceptions, everything that I have set down has been submitted to authority, and embodies the opinion of officers best qualified to judge—that is to say, of officers who have passed the best part of their lives with the men concerned. Even so I have no doubt that passages will be found that are open to dispute. Authorities disagree; estimates must vary, especially with regard to the relative worth of different classes; and one must always bear in mind that every company officer who is worth his salt is persuaded that there are no men like his own. It is a pleasing trait and an essential one. For it is the sworn confraternity between the British and Indian officer, and the strong tie that binds the sepoy to his Sahib which have given the Indian Army its traditions and prestige

All references and statistics concerning the Indian Army will be found to relate to the pre-war establishment; and no class of sepoy is included which has been enlisted for the first time since 1914. At the outbreak of war the strength of the Army in India was 76,953 British and 239,561 Indian. During the war 1,161,789 Indians were recruited. The grand total of all ranks sent overseas from India was 1,215,338. The casualties sustained by the force were 101,439. Races which never enlisted before enlisted freely, and the Indian Army List when published on the conclusion of Peace will be changed beyond recognition.

One or two classes I have omitted. The introduction of the Gujar, Meo, Baluchi and Brahui, for instance, as separate types, would be an error of perspective in a volume this size. It is hardly necessary to differentiate the Gujar from the Jat; the origin of the two races is much the same, and in appearance they are not always distinguishable. The Meo, too, approximates to the Merat. The Baluchi proper has practically ceased to enlist, and the sepoy who calls himself a Baluch is generally the descendant of immigrants. There is also a scattering of Brahuis in the Indian Army. They and the Baluchis are of the same stock, and are supposed to have come from Aleppo way, though in some extraordinary manner which nobody can understand the Brahuis have picked up a Dravidian accent.

It is difficult, too, to write of the Madrasi—Hindu, Mussalman, or Christian—as an entity apart. All I know of him is that in the Indian Sappers and Miners and Pioneer regiments, when he is measured with other classes, his British officer speaks of him as equal to the best.

The names of the officers to whom I am indebted would make a long list. I met them in camps, messes, trenches, dugouts, and in the open field. Some are old friends; others are unknown to me by name; many are unaware that they have contributed material for these sketches; and I can only thank them collectively for their help. For verification I have consulted the official handbooks of the Indian Army; and for certain of my references to the achievements of the Indian Army in France I am indebted to the semi-official history ("The Indian Corps in France," by Lieut.-Col. J. W. B. Merewether, C.I.E., and Sir Frederick Smith) published under the authority of the Secretary of State for India. One chapter, "The Drabi," I have taken almost bodily from my "Year of Chivalry," which also included the story of Wariam Singh; my thanks are due to the publishers, Messrs. Simpkin Marshall, for their permission to reprint it. For the account of the Jharwas I am indebted to an officer in a Gurkha regiment, who wishes to remain anonymous. For illustrations my thanks are due to General Holland Pryor, M.V.O., Major G. W. Thompson, and Lieut.-Cols. Alban Wilson, D.S.O., R. C. Wilson, D.S.O., M.C., F. L. Nicholson, D.S.O., M.C., H. M. W. Souter, W. H. Carter, E. R. P. Berryman, and Mr. T. W. H. Biddulph, C.I.E

Two Indian words occur frequently in these pages. They are *izzat* and *jiwan*, words that are constantly in the mouths of officers and sepoys. "Izzat" is best rendered by "honour" or "prestige"; "jiwan" means a "youngster," and is applied to the rank and file of the Indian Army without reference to age. I have kept the vernacular forms, as it is difficult to find exact English equivalents, and much that is homely and familiar in the words is lost in translation.

CONTENTS

LIST OF ILLUSTRATIONS

THE SEPOY

THE GURKHA

So much has been written of the Gurkha and the Sikh that officers who pass their lives with other classes of the Indian Army are tired of listening to their praises. Their fame is deserved, but the exclusiveness of it was resented in days when one seldom heard of the Mahratta, Jat, Dogra, and Punjabi Mussalman. But it was not the Gurkha's or the Sikh's fault if the man in the street puts them on a pedestal apart. Both have a very distinctive appearance; with the Punjabi Mussalman they make up the bulk of the Indian Army; and their proud tradition has been won in every fight on our frontiers. Now other classes, whose qualities were hidden, live in the public eye. The war has proved that all men are brave, that the humblest follower is capable of sacrifice and devotion: that the Afridi, who is outwardly the nearest thing to an impersonation of Mars, yields nothing in courage to the Madrasi Christian of the Sappers and Miners. These revelations have meant a general levelling in the Indian Army and the uplift of classes hitherto undeservedly obscure. At the same time the reputation of the great fighting stocks has been splendidly maintained.

The hillmen of Nepal have stood the test as well as the best. Ask the Devons what they think of the 1/9th Gurkhas who fought on their flank on the Hai. Ask Kitchener's men and the Anzacs how the 5th and 6th bore themselves at Gallipoli, and read Ian Hamilton's report. Ask Townshend's immortals how the 7th fought at Ctesiphon; and the British regiments who were at Mahomed Abdul Hassan and Istabulat what the 1st and 8th did in these hard-fought fights. Ask the gallant Hants rowers against what odds the two Gurkha battalions * forced the passage of the Tigris at Shumran on February 23rd. And ask the commander of the Indian Corps what sort of a fight the six Gurkha battalions † put up in France.

* 2nd and 9th.

† The 1/1st, 2/2nd, 2/3rd, 1/4th, 2/8th, and 1/9th.

Nothing could have been more strange to the Gurkha and more different from what his training for frontier warfare had taught him to expect than the conditions in Flanders. The first trenches the Gurkhas took over when they were pushed up to the front soon after their arrival in France were flooded and so deep that the little men could not stand up to the parapet. They were exposed to the most devastating fire of heavy artillery, trench-mortars, bombs, and machine guns. Parts of their trench were broken up and obliterated by the Hun Minnewerfers and became their graves. They hung on for the best part of a day and a night in this inferno, but in the end they were overwhelmed and driven out of the position, as happens sometimes with the best troops in the world. The surprising thing is that they became inured to this kind of warfare. Not only did they stand their ground, but in more than one assault they drove the Huns from their positions, and in September, 1915, the same battalion that had suffered so severely near Givenchy carried line after line of German trenches west of Martin du Pietre.

Those early months in France, when our troops, ill provided with bombs and trench-mortars and inadequately supported by artillery, were shattered by a machinery of destruction to which they could make little reply, were very much like hell. The soldier's dream of war had come, but in the form of a nightmare. Afterwards in Mesopotamia, the trench-fighting at El-Hannah and Sannaiyat was not much more inspiring. But the hour was to come when our troops had more than a sporting chance in a fight, and war became once more for the man at the end of the rifle something like his picture of the great game. The Gurkhas were severely tried in the ordeal by which this change was effected, and they played a stout part especially in the Tigris crossing, the honour of which they shared with the Norfolks; but, like the British Tommy in these trying times, they were always cheerful.

It is not the nature of any Sepoy to grouse. Patience and endurance is the heritage of all, but cheerfulness is most visible in the "Gurkh." He laughs like Atkins when the shells miss him, and he is never down on his luck. When the Turks were bombarding us on the Hai, I watched three delighted Gurkhas throwing bricks on the corrugated iron roof of a signaller's dug-out. A lot of stuff was coming over, shrapnel and high explosive, but the Gurkhas were so taken up with their little joke of scaring the signallers that the nearer the burst the better they were pleased. The signallers wisely lay "doggo" until one of the Gurkhas appeared at the door of the dug-out and gave the whole show away by a too expansive grin.

In France the element of shikar was eliminated. It would be affectation in the keenest soldier to pretend that he enjoyed the long-linked bitterness of Festubert, Givenchy, and Neuve Chapelle. But in Mesopotamia, especially after the crossing of the Tigris and the capture of Baghdad, there were many encounters in which one could think of war in the terms of sport. "There has been some shikar," is the Gurkha's way of describing indifferently a small scrap or a big battle. Neuve Chapelle was shikar. And it was shikar the other day when a Gurkha patrol by a simple stratagem surprised some mounted Turks. The stratagem succeeded. The Turks rode up unsuspectingly within easy range, but the Gurkhas did not empty a single saddle. Their British officer chaffed them on their bad shooting; but the havildar grinned and said, "At least a little shikar has taken place." That is the spirit. War is a kind of sublimated shikar. It is the mirror of the chase. The Gurkha is hunting when he is battle-mad, and sees red; and he is hunting when he glides alone through the grass or mud on a dark, silent night to stalk an enemy patrol. Following up a barrage on the Hai, the 1/9th were on the Turks like terriers. "Here, here, Sahib!" one of them called, and pointing to a bay where the enemy still cowered, pitched his bomb on a Turk's head with a grin of delight and looked round at a paternal officer for approval. Another was so excited that he followed his grenade into the trench before it had burst, and he and his Turk were blown up together.

The first time I saw Gurkhas in a civilized battle was at Beit Aieesa, where the little men were scurrying up and down the trenches they had just taken, with blood on their bayonets and clothes, bringing up ammunition and carrying baskets of bombs as happy and keen and busy as ferrets. They had gone in and scuppered the Turk before the barrage had lifted. They had put up a block and were just going to bomb down a communication trench. I saw one of

HAVILDAR CHANDRADHOJ (RAI).

To face p. 6]

TEKBAHADUR GHOTAM (KHAS).

To face p. 6.]

them pull up the body of a British Tommy who had been attached to the regiment as a signaller and was bombed into a mess. The Gurkha patted him on the shoulder and disappeared behind the traverse without a word.

The Gurkha fights as he hunts. Parties of them go into the jungle to hunt the boar. They beat the beast up and attack him with kukris when he tries to break through their line. It is a desperate game, and the casualties are a good deal heavier than in pig-sticking. The Gurkha's attitude to the Turk or the Hun is his attitude to the boar. There is no hostility or hate in him, and he is a cheerful, if a grim, fighter. There was never a Gurkha fanatic. The Magar or Gurung does not wish to wash his footsteps in the blood of the ungodly. To the righteous or the unrighteous stranger he is alike indifferent. There is no race he would wish to extirpate, and he has few prejudices and no hereditary foes. When his honour or interest is touched he is capable of rapid primitive reprisals, but he does not as a rule brood or intrigue. His outlook is that of a healthy boy. There is no person so easy to get on with as the "Gurkh." The ties of affection that bind him to his regimental officers are very intimate indeed. When the Sahib goes on leave trekking, or shooting, or climbing, he generally takes three or four of the regiment with him. I have often met these happy hunting-parties in and beyond the Himalayas. I have a picture in my mind of a scene by the Woolar Lake in Kashmir. The Colonel of a Gurkha regiment is sitting in a boat waiting for a youth whom he has allowed to go to a village on some errand of his own. The Colonel has waited two hours. At last the youth appears, all smiles, embracing a pumpkin twice the size of his head. No rebuke is administered for the delay. The youth squats casually in the boat at his Colonel's feet, and as he cuts the pumpkin into sections, makes certain unquotable comments on the village folk of Kashmir. As the pair disappear across the lake over the lotus leaves I hear bursts of laughter.

The relations between officers and men are as close as between boys and masters on a jaunt together out of school, and the Gurkha no more thinks of taking advantage of this when he returns to the regiment than the English schoolboy does when he returns to school. It is part of his jolly, boyish, uncalculating nature that he is never on the make. In cantonments, when any fish are caught or any game is shot, the first-fruits find their way to the mess. No one knows how it comes. The orderly will simply tell you that the men brought it. Perhaps after a deal of questioning the shikari may betray himself by a fatuous, shy, bashful grin.

The Gurkha does not love his officer because he is a Sahib, but because he is his Sahib, and the officer has to prove that he is his Sahib first, and learn to speak his language and understand his ways. A strange officer coming into a Gurkha regiment is not adopted into the Pantheon at once. He has to qualify. There may be a period of suspicion; but once accepted, he is served with a fidelity and devotion that are human and dog-like at the same time. I do not emphasize the exclusive attachment of the Gurkha to his own Sahib as an exemplary virtue; it is a fault, though it is the defect of a virtue. And it is a peculiarly boyish fault. It is the old story of magnifying the house to the neglect of the school. Infinite prestige comes of it; and this is to the good. But prestige is often abused. Exclusiveness does not pay in a modern army. In the organism of the ideal fighting machine the parts are compact and interdependent; and it would be a point to the good if every Gurkha were made to learn Hindustani and encouraged to believe that there are other gods besides his own.

When one hears officers in other Indian regiments disparage the Gurkha, as one does sometimes, one may be sure that the root of the prejudice lies in this exclusiveness. I have heard it counted for vanity, indifference, disrespect. It is even associated, though very wrongly, with the eminence, or niche apart, which he shares in popular estimation with the Sikh. But the Gurkha probably knows nothing about this niche. He is a child of nature. His clannishness is very simple indeed. He frankly does not understand a strange Sahib. Directly he tumbles to it that anything is needed of him he will lend a hand, but having no very deeply-ingrained habit of reverence for caste in the abstract apart from his devotion to the proved individual, he may appear sometimes a little neglectful in ceremony. But no Sahib with a grain of imagination or understanding in him will let the casual habits of the little man weigh in the balance against his grit and gameness, his loyalty, and his splendid fighting spirit. I am always suspicious of the officer who depreciates the Gurkha. He is either sensitively vain, or dull in reading character, or jealous of the dues which he thinks have been diverted from some other class to which he is personally attached.

This last infirmity one can understand and forgive. It grows out of an officer's attachment to his men. It is present sometimes in the British officers who command Gurkhas. Indeed, a man who after a year's service with any class of Sepoy is so detached and impartial in mind as not to find peculiar and distinctive virtues in his own men, ought not to be serving in the Indian Army at all. I remember once hearing a subaltern in a very obscure regiment discussing his class company. The battalion had not seen service for at least three generations, and everyone took it for granted that they would "rat" the first time they heard a shot fired. But the boy was full of "bukh."

"By Jove!" he said, "our fellows are simply splendid, the best plucked crowd in the Indian Army, and so game. . . . Oh no! they've never been in action, but you should just see how they lay one another out at hockey."

Before the war one would have smiled inwardly at this "encomium," if one could have preserved one's outward countenance, but Armageddon, the corrective of exclusiveness and pride, has taught us that gallantry resides under the most unlikely exteriors. It has taught us to look for it there. Anyhow the boy had the right spirit even if his faith were founded in illusion; for it is through these ties of mutual loyalty that the spirit of the Indian Army is strong.

The devotion of the Sepoy to his officer is common to most, perhaps to all, classes of the Indian Army. In some of the Gurkha battalions it is usual for two of the men to mark their Sahib when he goes into action, to follow him closely, and if he falls, to look after him and bring him back whether wounded or dead. This is a tacitly understood and quite unofficial arrangement, and the officer knows no more about his self-appointed guard than the hero or villain of melodrama about the detective who dogs his footsteps in the street. In France a British officer in a Gurkha regiment knocked out by shell-shock opened his eyes to find his orderly kneeling over him fanning the flies off his face. He lost consciousness again. When he came to the Gurkha was still fanning him, and the tears were rolling down his cheeks.

"Why are you crying, 'Tegh Bahadur?'" he said; "I am not badly hit."

"I am crying, Sahib," he said, "because my arm is gone, and I am no more able to fight." And with a nod he indicated the wound. The shell that had stunned the Sahib had carried off the orderly's forearm at the elbow.

The Medical Officer will tell you that the Gurkha is the pluckiest little fellow alive. In hospital he will go on smoking and chatting to you when he is dying, fighting his battles over again. I remember a Gurkha in an ambulance at Sinn pointing his index finger, which was hanging by a tendon, as he described the attack. During a cholera outbreak in 1916 among the Nepalese troops garrisoning the Black Mountains frontier a Gurkha, who was evidently *in extremis*, was being carried by his Major and another officer to a bit of rising ground where there was some shade and a little breeze. When in an interval of consciousness he opened his eyes and saw two Sahibs carrying him, he tried to raise himself to the salute, but fell back in a half faint. "You must pardon me, Sahib," he said, "but owing to weakness I am unable to salute." The Major told him to lie still. "We are taking you to a cool place," he explained. "Now you must be quick and get well." The Gurkha answered with a faint smile, "Now that your honours have honoured me by carrying me, I shall quickly get well." In a few minutes he died.

The Gurkha is not given to the neatly turned speech, the apt phrase, and one might search one's memory a long time before one recalled a compliment similar to this one spoken in simple sincerity by a dying man. The arts of conciliation are not practised where he camps. There is a delightful absence of the courtier about him, and he could not make pretty speeches if he tried. The "Our Colonel Sahib shot remarkably well, but God was merciful to the birds" story is told of a very different race. If a colonel of Gurkhas shoots really badly, his orderly will probably be found doubled up with mirth. The few comments of the Gurkha that stick in the mind are memorable in most instances for some crudeness, or misconception, or for a primitive, and not infrequently a somewhat gruesome, sense of humour. One meets many types, but the average "Gurkh," though observant, is not as a rule quick at the uptake. I heard a characteristic story of one, Chandradhoj, a stalwart Limbu of Eastern Nepal. It was in November last year, in the days of trench warfare. His Colonel had sent him from the Sannaiyat trenches to Arab Village to have his boots mended, and when he was returning in the evening the Turks got it into their heads that a relief was taking place, and put in a stiff bombardment, paying special attention to the road. Chandradhoj got safely back through this. When the Colonel met him in the evening passing his dug-out he stopped him and asked him how he had fared.

"Well, you've got back all right," he said. "You wern't hit!"

"No, Sahib, I was not hit. I came back in artillery formation."

One could see him solemnly stepping aside a few paces from the road, the prescribed distance from the imaginary sections on the left or right. These were the Sahib's orders at such times, he would argue, and there must be salvation in the rite.

The Gurkha sees what he sees, and his visual range is his mental range. At Kantara he only saw the desert, and the desert was sand. Other conditions beyond the horizon, an oasis for instance, were inconceivable. He tried to get it out of his Sahib how and where the Bedouin lived who came into Kantara Post. He thought they lived in holes in the sand, but what they ate he could not imagine. When they came into the Post looking wretched and miserable he gave them chapattis. "But, Sahib," he asked, "what could they have eaten before we came other than sand?"

One is never quite sure what will move a Gurkha to laughter. He grins at things which tickle a child's fancy, and he grins at things which make the ordinary man feel very sick inside. When the Turk abandoned Sinn in May, 1916, we occupied the position. The advance lay over the month-old battlefield of Beit Aieesa, and the enemy's dead were lying everywhere in a very unpleasant stage of dissolution. Suddenly the grimness of the scene was disturbed by explosive bursts of laughter. It was the Gurkhas. "Well, what is the joke? What are you laughing at?" an officer asked them. "Look, Sahib!" one of them said. "The devils are melting." Only he used a much more impolite word than "devil," for which we have no translation.

The Gurkha has not a very high estimate of

the value of life. A few years ago, when Rugby football was introduced in a certain battalion, there was an unfortunate casualty soon after the first kick-off. One of the men, collared by his Sahib, broke his neck on the hard ground, and was killed stone-dead. The incident sealed the fate of Association in the regiment, and Rugby became the vogue from that hour. "This is something like a game," they said, "when you kill a man every time you play."

The Gurkha would not be such a fine fighter if he had not a bit of the primitive in him. Several years ago two companies of a Gurkha battalion, who were holding a post in a frontier show, were bothered by snipers at night. The shots came from a clump of bushes on the edge of a blind nullah full of high brushwood, which for some reason it was inadvisable to picquet. Here was an excellent chance of shikar, and a havildar and four men asked if they might go out at night and stalk the Pathans. They were allowed to go, the conditions being that they were to go bare-footed, they were not to take rifles, and they were to do the work with the kukri. Also they were to stay out all night, as they would certainly be shot by the sentries of other regiments if they tried to come in. Only one sniper's bullet whizzed into camp that night. The next morning the havildar entered the mess while the officers were breakfasting. He came in with his left hand behind his back and saluted.

"Sahib," he said, "two of the snipers have been killed."

"That's good, havildar," the Colonel said. "But how do you know that you got them? Are they lying there, or have their brothers taken them away?"

The havildar, grinning broadly, produced a Pathan's head, and dumped it on the breakfast table. "The other is outside," he said. "Shall I bring it in?"

The Gurkha is good at this kind of night-work; he has the nerve of a Highlander and the stealth of a leopard. His great fault in a general attack is that he does not know when to stop. Without his Sahib he would not survive many battles. And that is why the casualties are so heavy in regiments when the British officers fall early in the fight. When the Gurkhas were advancing at Beit Aiseesa, I heard an officer in a Sikh regiment say, "Little blighters.

They're always scurrying on ahead, and if you don't look after them they will make a big salient and bite off more than they can chew." This is exactly what happened, though with the Turkish guns as a bait, guns which they took and lost afterwards by reason of the offending salient, they would not have been human if they had held back.

The Gurkha battalions, as everybody knows, have permanent cantonments in the hills, and do not move about like other regiments from station to station. Most of them have their wives and families in the lines, and in the leave season they get away for a time to their homes in Nepal. In peace the permanent cantonment with its continuity of home life is a privilege; but in the war the Gurkhas, like every other class of sepoy, have had to bear with a weariness of exile which it is difficult for any one but their own officers to understand. It is true of the Gurkha, as of the Indian of the plains, that he gives up more when he leaves his home to fight in a distant country than the European. The age-worn traditions and associations which make up homeliness for him, the peculiar and cherished routine, cannot be translated overseas. And it must be remembered that the sepoy has not the same stimulus as we have. It is true that he is a soldier, and that it is his business to fight, and that he is fighting his Sahib's enemy. That carries him a long way. But he does not see the Hun as his Sahib sees him, as an intolerable, blighting incubus which he must cast off or die. One appreciates his cheerfulness in exile all the more when one remembers this.

On a transport this summer in Basra, Asbahadur, a young Gurung from Western Nepal was pointed out to me. He had just come home from leave. He had six weeks in India, but there was the depôt to visit first. He had to pick up his kit and draw his pay, and by the time he had got to his village, Kaski Pokhri, on the Nepal frontier, sixteen days hard going from Gorakhpur in the U.P., he found that he had only four days at home before he must start off again to catch his steamer at Bombay. But he had seen his family, his house, his crops, the barn that had to be repaired, the familiar stretch of jungle and stream. He had dumped his money in the only place where money is any good; and he had seen that all was well.

He had learned, too, that it was well with

his young brother, who had run away from home to join the army, as so many young Gurkhas did at the beginning of the war,—literally "running" for the best part of two nights and days, only a short neck ahead of his pursuing parents, who had now forgiven him.

There is conscription in Nepal now and there is no need for the young men to run away. Asbahadur told me that he had met very few young men of his age near his home. In his village the women were doing the work, as they were in France, and as he understood was the case in the Sahib's country. The garrisoning of India by the Nepalese troops had depleted the county of youth. You only met old men and cripples and boys. Early in the war the Nepal Durbar came forward with a splendid offer of troops, which we were quick to accept. Thousands of her best, including the Maharaja's *Corps de garde*, poured over the frontier into Hindustan, and released many regular battalions for service overseas. They have fought on the frontier, and taken their part in policing the border from the Black Mountains on the north to as far south as the territory of the Mahsuds.

There are three main divisions of Gurkhas:

the Magar and Gurung of Central and Western Nepal, indistinguishable except for a slight accent; the Limbu and Rai of Eastern Nepal; and the Khattri and Thakur, who are half Aryan. The Magars and Gurungs are the most Tartar-like, short, with faces flat as scones. The Limbu and Rai physiognomy assimilates more with the Chinese. In the Khattri and Thakur, or Khas Gurkhas as they are called by others, though they do not accept the term, the Hindu strain is distinguishable, though the Mongol as a rule is predominant. They are the descendants of Brahmans or Rajputs and Gurkha women; hence the opprobrious "khas," or "fallen." But it is a blend of nobility—a proud birthright. It is only the implication of the "fall" they resent, —for these marriages were genuine but for the narrow legislation of orthodoxy and caste. Before the war it was taken as a matter of course by some that the streak of plainsman in the mountaineer must imply a softening of the national fibre, but the war has proved them as good as the best. In the crossing of the Tigris at Shumran, the miniature Mesopotamian Gallipoli, the Khas (9th Gurkhas) shared the honours in full with the Magars and Gurung (2nd Gurkhas);

but long before that any suspicion of inferiority had been dissipated.

It is difficult to differentiate the different classes, but the Khas Gurkha is probably the most intelligent. In the Limbu and the Rai there are sleeping fires. They are as fastidious about their honour as the Pathan and the Malay, and when any sudden and grim poetic justice is exacted in blood in a Gurkha regiment the odds are that one or the other are at the bottom of it. The Magars and the Gurung are the basic type, the "everyman" among Gurkhas, the backbone in numbers of the twenty battalions. As regards pluck there is nothing to choose between any of them, and if one battalion goes further than another the extra stiffening is the work of the British officers.

One's impression of the Gurkha in war and peace is of an almost mechanical smartness, movements as quick and certain as the click of a rifle bolt. Soldiering is a ritual among them. You may mark it in the way they pitch camp, solemnly, methodically, driving in each peg as if it were an ordained rite. They have learnt it all by rote. They could do it as easily in their sleep. And the discipline has stood the shock of seismic disturbance. In the Dharmsala earthquake of 1905 the quarter guard of the 2/8th Gurkhas turned out and saluted their officer with the same clockwork precision, when their bungalow had fallen like a house of cards. They had escaped by a miracle, and half the regiment had been killed, or maimed, or buried alive.

But remove the Gurkha from the atmosphere of barracks and camps and the whole ritual is forgotten like a dream. Out on shikar, or engaged in any work away from the battalion, he becomes his casual self again. But the guest of a Gurkha regiment does not see this side of him. I have memories of the men called into the mess and standing round like graven images, the personality religiously suppressed, the smile tardily provoked if Generals or strange Sahibs are present. A boy, with a smooth, round, innocent face, as still and as expressionless as if he had been hypnotized. Next him a man with the face of a bonze. Another with an expression of ferocity asleep and framed in benevolence. Passion has drawn those deep lines at right angles with the mouth. They are scars of the spirit—often enough now in the same setting as dints of lead and steel.

You get these faces in Gurung, Magar, Limbu, Khas, and Rai. But differentiation is profitless and often misleading, whether as regards the outward or inward man. I heard an almost heated discussion as to relative values by officers, who should know best, terminated by an outsider with the laconic comment, "They are all dam good at chivying chickens." As to this all were agreed. And the remark called up another picture—the Gurkha returning from a punitive raid against a cut-throat tribe, smothered in spoil and accoutrements, three carpets under one saddle, and the little man on top with chickens under each arm, and strung as thick as cartridges to his belt and bandolier.

THE SIKH

It has often been said that the Indian Army has kept Sikhism alive. War is a conserver of the Khalsa, peace a dissolvent. When one understands how this is so, one has grasped what Sikhism has done for the followers of the faith, and why the Sikh is different in habit and thought from his Hindu and Muhammadan neighbour, though in most cases he derives from the same stock.

The Sikhs are a community, not a race. The son of a Sikh is not himself a Sikh until he has taken the pahul, the ceremony by which he is admitted into the Khalsa, the community of the faithful. It would take volumes to explain exactly what initiation means for him. But the important thing to understand is that the convert, in becoming a Sikh, is not charged with a religious crusade. There is no bigotry in the faith that has made a Singh of him. His baptism by steel and "the waters of life" only means that he has gained prestige by admission into a

To face p. 26.] THE SIKH.

military and spiritual brotherhood of splendid traditions.

Guru Nanak (1469–1539), the founder of the sect, was a man of peace and a quietist. He only sought to remove the cobwebs that had overgrown sectarian conceptions of God. He could not in his most prophetic dreams have foreseen the bearded, martial Sikh whom we know to-day. This is the Govindi Sikh, the product of the tenth Guru, that inspired leader of men who welded his followers into the armed fraternity which supplanted the Moguls and became the dominant military class of the Punjab.

It was persecution that made the Sikh what he is—not theological conviction. Dogma was incidental. The rise of the Khalsa was a political movement. The thousands of Jat yeomen who joined the banner accepted the book with the sword. To make a strong and distinctive body of them, to lift them above the Hindu ranks, to convert a sect into a religion, to give them a cause and a crusade was Govind's work. It was he who consolidated the Sikhs by giving them prestige. He instituted the Khalsa, or the commonwealth of the chosen, into which his disciples were initiated by the ceremony of the pahul. He swept away ritual, abolished caste, and ordained that every Sikh should bear the old Rajput title of Singh, or Lion, as every Govindi Sikh does to this day. He also gave national and distinctive traits to the dress of his people, ordaining that they should carry a sword, dagger, and bracelet of steel, don breeches instead of a loin-cloth, and wear their hair long and secured in a knot by a comb. He it was who grafted the principles of valour, devotion, and chivalry on the humble gospel of Nanak, and introduced the national salutation of "Wah Guru ji ka Khalsa! Wa Guru ji ki Futteh!"—"Hail to the Khalsa! Victory to God"—a chant that has dismayed the garrison of many a doomed trench held by the Turk and the Hun.

> "The Sikhs of Govind shall bestride horses,
> And bear hawks upon their hands;
> The Turks who behold them shall fly;
> One shall combat a multitude,
> And the Sikh who thus perishes shall be blessed for ever." *

It was odd that the Arabs in Mesopotamia should have called the Sikh "the black lion," † bearing witness to the boast that every member of the Khalsa when he puts on the consecrated steel and adopts the title of Singh is lionised in

* The Tunkha Nameh of Guru Govind.

† Sabaa aswad.

the most literal sense of the word and becomes the part in fact as well as in name.

War is a necessary stimulus for Sikhism. In the reaction of peace the Sikh population dwindles. It was in the struggle with Islam, during the ascendency of Ranjit Singh, in the two wars against the British, and after in the Mutiny, when the Sikhs proved our loyal allies, that the Khalsa was strongest. Without the incentive to honour and the door open to military service the ineradicable instincts of the Hindu reassert themselves. Fewer jiwans come forward and take the pahul; not only is the community weakened by lack of disciples, but many who hold fast to the form let go the spirit; ritual, idolatry, superstition, exclusiveness, and caste, the old enemies to the reformed religion, creep in again; the aristocracy of honour lapses into the aristocracy of privilege. Then the Brahman enters in, and the simple faith is obscured by all manner of un-Sikh-like preoccupations. Sikhism might have fallen back into Hinduism and become an obscure sect if it had not been for the Indian Army. But here the insignia of Guru Govind have been maintained, and his laws and traditions. The class regiments and class-company regiments have preserved not merely the outward observances; they have kept alive the inward spirit of the Khalsa. Thus it is that the Sikh has more class feeling than any other sepoy, and more pride in himself and his community. Govind set the lion stamp on him as he intended. By his outward signs he cannot be mistaken—by his beard, the steel bracelet on his wrist, his long knotted hair, or if that is hidden, by the set of his turban, above all by his grave self-respect. The casual stranger can mark him by one or all of these signs, but there is a subtler physical distinction in expression and feature that you cannot miss when you know the Sikh well. This is quite independent of insignia. It is as marked in a boy without a hair to his chin as in an old campaigner. This also is Govind's mark, the sum of his influence inscribed on the face by the spirit. A great tribute this to the genius of the Khalsa, when one remembers that the Sikh is not a race apart, but comes of the same original stock as most of his Hindu and Muhammadan neighbours in the Punjab, and that Govind, his spiritual ancestor, only died two hundred years ago.

Amongst all the races and castes that have been caught up into the Khalsa, by far the most important in influence and numbers is the Jat. Porus was probably of the race. When Alexander, impressed by his gallantry, asked him what boon he might confer, he demanded "to be treated like a king"—a very, Sikh-like speech. The Sikh soldier is the Jat sublimated, and the bulk of the Sikhs in the Indian Army are of Jat origin. Authorities differ as to the derivation of the Jats, but it is commonly believed that they and the Rajputs are of the same Scythian origin, and that they represent two separate waves of invasion; and this is borne out by their physical resemblance and by a general similarity in their communal habits of life. The Jat, so long as he remains a Hindu, is called Jāt (pronounced Jā-āt), while the Jat who has adopted Sikhism is generally referred to as Jăt (pronounced Jŭt). The spelling is the same, and to the uninitiated this is a constant source of confusion. The difference in pronunciation arose from a subtlety of dialect, it being customary in the part of the Punjab where Sikhs preponderate to shorten the long Ā of the Hindi.

The Jat is the backbone of the Punjab. From his Scythian ancestors is derived the same stubborn fibre that stiffens the Punjabi cultivator, whatever changes he may have suffered by influence of caste or creed, whether he be Hindu, Muhammadan, or Sikh. The admitted characteristics of the Jat are stubbornness, tenacity, patience, devotion, courage, discipline and independence of spirit fitly reconciled; add to these the prestige and traditions of the Khalsa and you have the ideal Sikh.

I say "the ideal Sikh," for without the contributory influences you may not get the type as Govind conceived it. The ideal Sikh is the happy Sikh, the Sikh who is content with the place he occupies in his cosmos, who respects and believes in his superior officers, who does not consider himself unjustly treated, and who has received no injury to his self-esteem. For the virtuous ingredients in his composition are subject to reaction. When he fancies he is wronged, he broods. The milk in him becomes gall. The "waters of life" stirred by steel, his baptismal draught, take on an acid potency. "I'd rather command Sikhs than any other class of sepoy," a brigadier told me, and he had commanded every imaginable class of sepoy for twenty years, "but they must be happy Sikhs," he added. The brooding or intriguing Sikh is a nuisance and a danger.

The pick of the Khalsa will be found in the class regiments and class company regiments to which the Sikhism of to-day owes its conservation, vigour, and life. The 14th Sikhs were raised at Ferozepore in 1846; the 15th at Ludhiana in the same year; the 45th Rattray's Sikhs in 1856 for service among the Sonthals; the 35th and 36th Sikhs in 1887, the 47th in 1901. The 15th, the oldest Sikh battalion, and the 47th, the latest raised, were the first to be given the opportunity of showing the mettle of the Khalsa in a European war. The 47th, who were not raised till 1901, earned as proud a record as any in France, distinguishing themselves from the day in October, 1914, when, with the 20th and 21st Sappers and Miners, they cleared the village of Neuve Chapelle after some Homeric hand-to-hand fighting in the houses and streets, to the desperately stubborn advance up the glacis to the German trenches on April 26, 1915, in the second battle of Ypres, when the regiment went in with eleven British and ten Indian officers and 423 other ranks, of whom but two British and two Indian officers and 92 rank and file mustered after the action. The 15th Sikhs, one of the two earliest-raised Sikh battalions, were the first to come into action in France, and they maintained a high-level reputation for gallantry all through the campaign. The story of Lieutenant Smyth and his ten Sikh bombers at Festubert is not likely to be forgotten. Smyth and two sepoys were the only two survivors of this gallant band who passed by a miracle, crawling over the dead bodies of their comrades, through a torrent of lead, and carried their bombs through to the first line. Smyth was awarded the V.C., Lance-Naik Mangal Singh the Indian Order of Merit, and every sepoy in the party the Indian Distinguished Service Medal. Two of these men belonged to the 45th Sikhs, four to the 19th Punjabis. And here it should be remembered that the Sikhs earned a composite part of the honour of nearly every mixed class-company regiment in France; of the Punjabi regiments, for instance, and of the Frontier Force Rifle battalions, in which the number of Sikh companies varies from one to four, not to mention the Sappers and Miners. It was in the very first days of the Indians' *début* in France that a Sikh company of the 57th Rifles earned fame when it was believed that the line must have given way, holding on all through the night against repeated counter-attacks, though the Germans were past them on both flanks. As for the Sappers, the story of Dalip Singh is pure Dumas. This fire-eater helped his fallen officer, Lieut. Rail-Kerr, to cover, stood over him and kept off several parties of Germans by his fire. On one occasion—a feat almost incredible, but well established—he was attacked by twenty of the enemy, but beat them all off and got his officer away.*

It is in "sticking it out" that the Sikh excels. No one will deny his *élan*; yet *élan* is not so remarkably and peculiarly his as the dogged spirit of resistance that never admits defeat, the spirit that carried his ancestors through the long ordeal by fire in their struggle with the Moguls. It is in defensive action that the Sikhs have won most renown, fighting it out against hopeless, or almost hopeless odds, as at Arrah and Lucknow in the Mutiny, and in the Tirah campaign at Saraghiri on the Samana ridge. The defence of the little house at Arrah by Rattray's (the 45th) Sikhs was one of the most glorious episodes of the Indian Mutiny, and the

* "The Indian Corps in France," by Lieut.-Colonel J. W. B. Merewether, C.I.E., and Sir Frederick Smith.

story of the Sikh picket at Saraghiri will live as long in history. The whole garrison of the post, twenty-one men of the 36th Sikhs, a battalion lately raised and then in action for the first time, fell to a man in its defence. The Afridis admitted the loss of two hundred dead in the attack. As they pressed in on all sides in overwhelming numbers the Sikhs kept up their steady fire for six hours, until the walls of the post fell. The last of the little band perished in the flames as he defended the guard-room door, and shot down twenty of the assailants before he succumbed.

Strangely enough, these two regiments, the 36th and 45th Sikhs, to whom we owe two of the most enduring examples in history of "sticking it out," fought side by side on the Hai in an action which called for as high qualities of discipline and endurance under reverse as any that was fought in Mesopotamia. The Sikhs lived up to their tradition. Both regiments went over the parapet in full strength and were practically annihilated. Only 190 effectives came out of the assault; only one British officer returned unwounded. The 45th on the right were exposed to a massed counter-attack. A British officer was seen to collect his men and close in on the Turks in the open; he and his gallant band were enveloped and overwhelmed. So, too, in Gallipoli the 14th Sikhs, who saved Allahabad in the Mutiny and immortalized themselves with Havelock in the march on Lucknow and the defence of the Residency, displayed their old spirit. When they had fought their way through the unbroken wire at Gully Ravine (June 4, 1915) and taken three lines of trenches, they hung on all day, though they had lost three-fourths of their effectives, and every British officer but two was killed.

But I must tell the story of Wariam Singh, a Jat Sikh of a Punjabi regiment; it was told me by one Zorowar Singh, his comrade, in France. "You heard of Wariam Singh, Sahib," he asked —"Wariam Singh, who would not surrender?"

Wariam Singh was on leave when the regiment was mobilized, and the news reached him in his village. It was a very hot night. They were sitting by the well, and when Wariam Singh heard that the —— Punjabis were going to Wilayat to fight for the Sircar against a different kind of white man, he said that, come what might, he would never surrender. He made a vow then and there, and, contrary to all regimental discipline, held by it.

I can picture the scene—the stencilled shadows of the kikar in the moonlight, the smell of baked flour and dying embers, the almost motionless group in a ring like birds on the edge of a tank, and in the background the screen of tall sugar-cane behind the dry thorn hedge. The village kahne-wallah (recounter of tales) would be half chanting, half intoning, with little tremulous grace-notes, the ballad about "Wa-ar-button Sahib," or Jân Nikalsain, when the lumbardar from the next village would appear by the well and portentously deliver the message.

The scene may have flickered before the eyes of Wariam Singh, lying stricken beside his machine-gun, just as the cherry blossom of Kent is said to appear to the Kentish soldier. The two English officers in his trench had fallen; the Germans had taken the trenches to the left and the right, and they were enfiladed up to the moment when the final frontal wave broke in. The order came to retire, but Wariam Singh said, "I cannot retire, I have sworn"; and he stood by his machine-gun.

"If he had retired no doubt he would have

been slain. Remaining he was slain, but he slew many," was Zorowar Singh's comment.

Afterwards the trench was taken back, and the body of Wariam Singh was found under the gun. The corpses of the Germans lay all round "like stones in a river bed."

The disciples of Govind comprise many classes other than the Jat, of whom there are some thirty main clans. There are Sikhs of Brahman and Rajput descent, and a number of tribes of humbler origin. The Jat stands first in respect to honour and numbers; apart from him, it is the humbler classes who have contributed most weight to the fighting arms of the community. The Brahman-, Rajput-, and Khatri-descended Sikhs do not enlist freely.

The 48th Pioneers are recruited almost entirely from Labanas, a tribe whose history goes back to the beginning of time. There are Labanas, of course, who are not Sikhs. The Raja of the community is a Hindu and lives at Philibit, and there are Labana hillmen about Simla, farmers in the Punjab, traders in the Deccan and Bombay, and owners of ships; but I have no doubt that the pick of them are those that have enlisted in the Khalsa. The Labanas were soldiers at least two thousand years before Govind, and according to tradition formed the armed transport of the Pandavas and brought in the fuel (labanke—a kind of brushwood, hence the tribal name) for the heroes of the Mahabharata. I heard this story from a Labana Sikh one night on the upper reaches of the Euphrates near Khan Baghdadi, when we were miles ahead of our transport and had rounded up a whole army of Turks. He told it me with such impressment that I felt it must be true, though no doubt there are spoilers of romance who would unweave the web.

Theoretically Sikhism acknowledges no caste; but in practice the Sikh of Jat or Rajput descent will not eat or drink with Sikhs drawn from the menial classes, though the lowest in the social scale have been tried and proved on the field, and shown themselves possessed of military qualities which, apart from caste prejudice, should admit them to an equal place in the brotherhood of the faithful. The Mazbhis are a case in point. The first of this despised sweeper class to attain distinction were the three whom Guru Govind admitted into the Khalsa as a reward for their fidelity and devotion when they rescued the body of Tegh Bahodur, the murdered ninth Guru, from the fanatical Moslem mob at Delhi. When Sikhism was fighting for its life, these outcasts were caught up in the wave of chivalry and "gentled their condition;" but as soon as the Khalsa were dominant in the Punjab the Mazbhis found that the equality their religion promised them existed in theory rather than fact. They occupied much the same position among the Jat- and Khattri-descended Sikhs as their ancestors, the sweepers, enjoyed amongst the Hindus. They were debarred from all privileges, and were at one time even excluded from the army. It fell to the British to restore the status of the Mazbhi, or rather to give him the opening by which he was able to re-establish his honour and self-esteem. The occasion was in the Mutiny of 1857, when we were in great need of trained sappers for the siege-work at Delhi. A number of Mazbhis who were employed at the time in the canal works at Madhopur were offered military service and enlisted readily. On the march to Delhi these raw recruits fought like veterans. They were attacked by the rebels, beat them off, and saved the whole of the ammunition and treasure. During the siege Neville Chamberlain wrote of them that "their courage amounted to utter recklessness of life." Eight of them carried the powder-bags to blow up the Kashmir Gate, under Home and Salkeld. Their names are inscribed on the arch to-day and have become historical. John Lawrence wrote of the deed as one of "deliberate and sustained courage, as noble as any that ever graced the annals of war."

The Mazbhis are recruited for the Sikh Pioneer regiments, the 23rd, 32nd, and 34th, sister regiments of whom one, or more, has been engaged in nearly every frontier campaign from Waziristan in 1860 to the Abor expedition in 1911. It was the 32nd who carried the guns over the Shandur Pass in the snow, in the march from Gilgit, and relieved the British garrison in Chitral. The 34th were among the earliest Indian regiments engaged in France, and the Mazbhis gained distinction in October, 1914, when they were pushed up to relieve the French cavalry, and the Sikh officers carried on the defence for a day and a night under repeated attacks when their British officers had fallen. Great, too, was the gallantry of the Indian officers of the regiment at Festubert (November, 1914), and the spirit of the ranks. Yet the

Mazbhis are still excluded from most privileges by the Khalsa. They are not eligible for the other Sikh class regiments. Nor are they acceptable in the cavalry or in other arms, for the aristocratic Jat Sikh, as a rule, refuses to serve with them. Yet you will find a sprinkling of Jat Sikhs in the Mazbhi Pioneer regiments—quick-witted, ambitious men usually, who are ready to make some sacrifice in the way of social prestige for the sake of more rapid promotion. The solid old Mazbhis, with all their sterling virtues, are not quick at picking up ideas. It is sometimes difficult to find men among them with the initiative to make good officers. Thus in a Mazbhi regiment the more subtle-minded Jat does not find it such a stiff climb out of the ranks.

It would be a mistake to think that the Jat Sikh is necessarily a better man in a scrap than the Mazbhi, though this is no doubt assumed as a matter of course by officers whose acquaintance with the Sikh is confined to the Jat. I shall never forget introducing a young captain in a Mazbhi regiment to a very senior Colonel on the Staff. The colonel in his early days had been a subaltern in the —th Sikhs, but had put in most of his life's work in "Q" Branch up at Simla, and did not know a great deal about the Sikh or any other sepoy. He turned to the young leader of Mazbhis, who is quite the keenest regimental officer I know, and said—

"Your men are Mazbhis, aren't they? But I suppose you have a stiffening of Jats."

The youngster's eyes glinted rage and he breathed fire.

"STIFFENING, sir? Stiffening of JATS! Our men are Mazbhis."

Stiffening was an unhappy word, and it stuck in the boy's gorge for weeks. To stiffen the Mazbhi,

> "to gild refined gold,
> To add another hue unto the rainbow,"

all come in the same catalogue of ridiculous excess. Stiffening! Why the man is solid concrete. It would take a stream of molten larva to make him budge. Or, as Atkins would say—

"He wants a crump on his blamed cokernut before he knows things is beginning to get a bit 'ot, and then he ain't sure."

It was to stiffen his men a bit, as they were all jiwans and likely to get a little flustered, that old Khattak Singh, Subadar of the 34th Sikh Pioneers, called "Left, right; right, left," as the regiment tramped into action at Dujaila; but the Mazbhi did not want stiffening. It is rather his part to contribute the inflexible element when there is fear of a bent or broken line. In the action at Jebel Hamrin, on March 25, 1917, when we tried to drive the Turks from a strong position in the hills, where they outnumbered us, the Mazbhis showed us how stiff they could be. They were divisional troops and for months they had been employed in wiring our line at night, —a wearing business, standing about for hours in the dark, under a blind but hot fire, casualties every night and never a shot at the Turk. So tired were they of being fired at without returning the enemy's fire that, when they got the chance at Jebel Hamrin and were rolling over visible Turks, for a long time they could not be induced to retire. The Turks were bringing off an enveloping movement which threatened our right. The order had been given for the retirement. But the Mazbhis did not, or would not, hear it. Somebody, I forget whether it was a British officer, or if it was an Indian officer after the British officers had all fallen, said that he would not retire without a written order. Ninety of them out of one hundred and fifty fell. Old Khattak Singh got back in the night, walked six miles to the hospital with seven wounds, one in his shoulder and two in his thigh, and said, "I had ninety rounds. I fired them all at the Turks and killed a few. Now I am happy and may as well lie up for a bit."

The Staff Colonel had a certain spice of humour, if little tact, and I think he rather liked the boy for his outburst in defence of his dear Mazbhis. To the outsider these little passages afford continual amusement. One has to mix with different regiments a long time before one can follow all the *nuances*, but it does not take long to realize to what extent the British officer is a partisan. Insensibly he suffers through his affections a kind of conversion. He comes to see many things as his men see them, even to adopt their own estimate of themselves in relation to other sepoys. And one would not have it otherwise. It speaks well for the qualities of the Indian soldier, for the courage, kindliness, loyalty, and faith with which he binds his British officer to his own community. It may be very narrow and wrong, but an Indian regiment is the better fighting unit for it. Better an enthusiasm that is sometimes ridiculous than a lukewarm attachment. The officer who does not think much of his jiwans will not go far with them. There are cases, of course, where pride runs riot and verges on snobbishness. I remember a subaltern who was shocked at the idea of his men playing hockey with a regiment recruited from a lower caste. And I once knew a field officer in a class regiment of Jat Sikhs who, I am sure, would have felt very uncomfortable if he had been asked to sit down at table with an officer who commanded Mazbhis. Yet, I am told, he was a fine soldier.

Fanatics of his kidney were happily rare. I use the past tense for they have gone with the best, and I am speaking generally of a school that has vanished. It may be resuscitated, but it will hardly be in our time. Too many of the old campaigners, transmitters of tradition, splendid fellows who lived for the regiment and swore by it, are dead or crippled, and the pick of the Indian Army Reserve has been reaped by the same scythe. The gaps have had to be filled so fast and from a material so unready that one meets officers now who know nothing about their sepoys, who do not understand their language and who are not even interested in them, youngsters intended for other walks of life who will never be impressed by the Indian soldier until they have first learnt to impress him.

THE PUNJABI MUSSALMAN

The "P. M.", or Punjabi Mussalman, is a difficult type to describe. Next to the Sikh, he makes up the greater part of the Indian Army. Yet, outside camps and messes, one hears little of him. The reason is that in appearance there is nothing very distinctive about him; in character he combines the traits of the various stocks from which he is sprung, and these are legion; also, as there are no P. M. class regiments, he is never collectively in the public eye.

Yet the P. M. has played a conspicuous part in nearly every action the Indian Army has fought in the war, and in every frontier campaign for generations; in gallantry, coolness, endurance, dependability, he is every bit as good as the best.

"Why don't you write about the P. M.?" a friend in the Nth asked me once. He was a major in a Punjabi regiment, and had grown grey in service with them.

We were standing on the platform of a flanking trench screened by sandbags from Turkish snipers, looking out over the marsh at Sannaiyat. Nothing had happened to write home about for six months, not since we delivered our third and bloodiest attack on the position on the 22nd April. The water had receded nearly a thousand yards since then. Our wire fences stood out high and dry on the alkaline soil. The blue lake seemed to stretch away into the interstices of the hills which in the haze looked a bare dozen miles away.

Two days before our last attack in April the water was clean across our front six inches deep, with another six inches of mud; on the 21st it was subsiding; on the 22nd the flooded ground was heavy, but it was decided that there was just a chance. So the assault was delivered. The Turkish front line was flooded; there was no one in it, and it was not until we had passed it that we were really in difficulties. The second line of trenches was neck deep in water; behind it there was a network of dug-outs and pits into which we floundered blindly. Beyond this, between the Turkish second and third lines, the mud was knee deep. The Highlanders, a composite battalion of

To face p 50.] THE PUNJABI MUSSALMAN.

the Black Watch and Seaforths, and the 92nd Punjabis, as they struggled grimly through, came under a terrific fire. It was here that their splendid gallantry was mocked by one of those circumstances which make one look darkly for the hand of God in war.

The breeches of their rifles had become choked and jammed with mud. The Jocks were tearing at them with their teeth, panting and sobbing, and choking for breath. They were almost at grips with the Turk, but could not return his fire.

The last action we fought for Kut was unsuccessful, but the gallantry of the men who poured into that narrow front through the marsh will become historic. The Highlanders hardly need praise. The constancy of these battalions has come to be regarded as a natural law. "The Jocks were magnificent," my friend said, "as they always are. So were the Indians."

And amongst the Indians were the P. Ms. There were other classes of sepoy who may have done as well, but the remnants of the three Indian battalions in this fight were mostly Punjabi Mussalmans. And here, as at Nasiriyeh, Ctesiphon and Kut-el-Amara, in Egypt and

France, at Ypres, Festubert and Serapeum, the P. M. covered himself with glory. The Jock, that sparing critic of men, had nothing but good words for him.

"Yes! Why don't you write about the P. M.?" the Major asked. One of the reasons why I had not written about the P. M. is that he is a very difficult person to write about. There is nothing very salient or characteristic about him; or rather, he has the characteristics of most other sepoys. To write about the P. M. is to write about the Indian Army. And that is why, to my friend's intense annoyance, the man in the street, who speaks glibly of Gurkha, Sikh, and Pathan, has never heard of him.

"Here's the old P. M. sweating blood," he said, "all through the show, slogging away, sticking it out like a good 'un, and as modest as you make 'em. Never bukhs; never comes up after a show and tells you what he has done. You don't know unless you see him. Old Shere Khan, our bomb havildar, was hit through both jaws on the 22nd. He got two bullets in the arm. Then he was shot in the lungs. But it was only when he got his fifth wound in the leg that he ceased to lead his men and limped back to the first-aid post. All our B. O.'s were down, but a doctor man with the Highlanders happened to see the whole thing. So Shere Khan was promoted."

The Major was bound to his P. Ms. with hoops of steel. It was the rifles with fixed bayonets slung from pegs between the sandbags that recalled Polonius' metaphor. It seemed more apt at Sannaiyat.

He introduced me to the Jemadar, Ghulam Ali, a man with a mouth like a rat-trap and remarkable for a kind of dour smartness. The end of his pagri was drawn out into a jaunty little tuft by the side of his kula. His long hair, oiled, but uncurled, fell down to the nape of his neck. Ghulam Ali, though shot through the forearm himself, had built up a screen of earth round his Sahib when he was severely wounded at the Wadi, stayed with him till dusk, helped him back to better cover, and then returned to the firing line to bring in a lance-naik on his shoulders.

There were very few of the old crowd left in the trenches. "These youngsters are mostly recruits," the Major explained, "but they are a good lot. I wish you could have seen Subadar

——," and he mentioned a man who had practically run a district in East Africa all on his own when there was no white man by. A tremendous character. "And Subadar-Major Farman Ali Bahadar. He got the D.S.M. when he was with us in Egypt, led a handful of his men across the open at Touffoum, and turned the Turkish flank very neatly. He got an I.O.M. at Sheikh Saad. And he led the regiment back at Sannaiyat when all the British officers were down. He was a Khoreshi, by the way."

A Khoreshi is a member of the tribe of the Prophet. A good Khoreshi is a man to be sought for and honoured, for his influence is great; but a bad Khoreshi among the P. Ms. is as big a nuisance as a Mir among Pathans.

"A kind of ecclesiastical dignitary," the Major explained, "a sort of Rural Dean. You will find men who funk him for reasons which have nothing to do with discipline; and if he pulls the wrong way it is the very devil."

The P. Ms. in the trenches were varied in type. There was nothing distinctive or showy about them, only they all looked workman-like; Sikh, Jat, and Punjabi Mussalman are mostly of common stock, and they assimilate so much in feature that it is sometimes difficult to distinguish between them. The P. Ms. ancestry may be Rajput, Jat, Gujar, Arab or Mogul. There are more than 400 tribes which he can derive from, and these are broken up into innumerable sects and sub-divisions. He does not pride himself on his class, but on his clan. The generic "izzat" of the P. M. is merged in the specific "izzat" of the Gakkar, Tiwana, Awan, or whatever he may be. "Punjabi Mussalman" is a purely official designation. And that is why the general public hears so little of him.

As a class he is a kind of Indian Everyman and comprises all. You will find among the P. Ms. every variety of type, from the big-boned Awan, stalwart of the Salt Range, to the thin-bearded little hillman of Poonch; from the Tiwanas, bloods of the Thal country who give us the pick of our cavalry and will not serve on foot, to the wiry Baluchi, who has forgotten the language and observances of his kinsmen over the border. You will find descendants of all the Muhammadan invaders of India, from the time of Mahmud of Ghazni in A.D. 1001, and of pre-Islamic invaders centuries before that, and of the converts of every considerable Moslem freebooter since. The recruiting officer encourages pride of race, which is generally accompanied with a soldierly bearing and pride in arms, though the oldest stock is not always the best. You will find among the P. Ms. Khoreshis and Sayads of the tribes of the Prophet and of Ali, Gakkars who will only give their daughters to Sayads, Ketwals who descended from Alexander the Great. The Bhatti are Pliny's Baternae. The Awans claim descent from the iconoclast Mahmud. At Sannaiyat I saw a Jungua of the Jhelum district who might have stood for a portrait of Disraeli. The true, or spurious, seed of the Moguls are scattered all over the Punjab, and there are scions of ancient Rajput stock like the Ghorewahas, who preserve their bards and are still half Hindus, and the Manj, who are too blue-blooded to follow the plough. But as a rule the P. M. has less frills than the Hindu of the same stock; he will lend a hand at any honest work, and falls easily into disciplinary ways.

What is it then that differentiates the Punjabi Mussalman? I put the case to my friend.

"Your P. M. comes from all stocks, has the same ancestor as the Jat, the Sikh, the Rajput, or the Pathan. Can you tell me exactly what being a P. M. does for him?"

The Major was unable to enlighten me fully. He told me what I had heard officers say of other classes of sepoy; only he left out all their faults.

"Personally, I think the P. M. is more human," he said. "He is not so proud as the ——, or so ambitious as the ——, or so mean as the ——, or so stupid as the ——. He is a cheery soul, and when he gets money he doesn't mind spending it. He is the most natural and direct of men, and there is no damned humbug about him. I remember old Fazal Khan pulling up a jiwan (youth) we had up, and who was being cross-examined in an inquiry about some lost ammunition. The youngster hedged, corrected himself, modified his statements, and generally betrayed his reluctance to come to the point. Fazal Khan's rebuke was characteristic. 'Judging distance ka mafik gawahi mut do!' he said ('Don't give your evidence as if you were judging distance at the range!'). He had a wholesome contempt for civilian ways. The regiment was giving a tamasha in the lines—an anniversary show—and one of our subalterns suggested putting up a row of flags all the way from the gate to the marquee. But Fazal Khan was not for it. 'No, sahib!' he said gravely, 'too civil ka mafik,' 'the sort of thing a civilian would do.' The old fellow is a soldier all through."

The Major's story gave me a glimmering of what it was that being a P. M. did for Fazal Khan and his brood. "There is no damned humbug about them,"—which was his way of saying that his friends neglect the arts of insinuation.

"There is something downright about the P. M. Even when he is mishandled, he is not mulish, only dispirited. And he'll do anything for the right kind of Sahib. Besides, look how he rolls up, recruiting is now better than ever—he is the backbone of the Indian Army."

A good "certifkit" and I think in the main true, though necessarily partial. But the Major was not literally accurate in saying that the P. M. is the backbone of the Indian Army. The Sikhs would have something to say to that, for 214 companies of infantry, including the class regiments, and forty squadrons of cavalry, are recruited entirely from the Khalsa, besides a large proportion of sappers and miners, and half the mountain batteries. The Gurkhas contribute twenty battalions of foot, but they serve only in the infantry. Taking infantry, cavalry, artillery and sappers, the P. M. in point of numbers is an easy second to the Sikh.*

There are, of course, Mussalman sepoys and sowars recruited from other provinces than the Punjab. Those from the United Provinces fall under the official designation of "Hindustani Mussalman," and need not be differentiated from the Muhammadans east of the Jumna. The same qualities may be discovered in any clan; the difference is only in degree; it is among the Punjabi Mussalmans that you will find the pick of Islam in the Indian Army.

Of quality it is difficult to speak. He is a bold man who would generalise upon the Indian Army, more especially upon the Punjab fighting stocks. The truth is that, if you pick the best of them and give them the same officers, there is nothing to choose between Sikh, Jat, and Punjabi Mussalman. Only you must be careful to choose your men from districts where they inherit the

* These statistics relate to the pre-war establishment of the Indian Army.

land and are not alien and browbeaten, but carry their heads high.

Why, then, if the P. M. is as good as the best, has he not been discovered by the man in the street? One reason I have suggested. You can shut your eyes in the Haymarket and conjure up an image of Gurkha, Sikh, or Pathan, but you cannot thus airily summon the P. M.—because he is Everyman, the type of all. Another source of his obscurity is the illogical nomenclature of the Indian Army. A class designation does not mean a class regiment. How many Baluchis proper are there in the so-called Baluchi regiments? Who gives a thought to the Dogras, P. Ms. and Pathans in the 51st, 52nd, 53rd, and 54th Sikhs, the Dekkani Mussalman in the Maharatta regiments, or the Dogras and P. Ms. in the 40th Pathans? Now the P. M. only exists in the composite battalions. He has no class regiment of his own. You may look in vain in the Army List for the 49th Gakkars, 50th Awans, or the 69th Punjabi Mussalmans. Hence it is that the P. M. swells the honour of others, while his own name is not increased.

Every boy in the street heard of the 40th Pathans at Ypres, but few knew that there were two companies of P. Ms. in the crowd—"as good as any of them," the Major said, "men who would stiffen any regiment in the Indian Army."

And when it is generally known that the —— Sikhs were first into the Turkish trenches on the right bank at Sheikh Saad and captured the two mountain guns, nobody is likely to hear anything of the P. M. company who was with them, a composite part of the battalion.

The Major's men had been complimented for every action they had been in, and this was the scene of their most desperate struggle. But there was little to recall the Sannaiyat of April —only an occasional bullet whistling overhead, or cracking against the sandbags. Instead of mud a thin dust was flying and the peaceful birds stood by the edge of the lake.

I wished the P. M. could have his Homer. Happily he is not concerned with the newspaper paragraph. Were the Press to discover him it is doubtful if he would hear of it. He enlists freely. He is such an obvious fact, stands out so saliently wherever the Indian Army is doing anything, looms so large everywhere, that it has probably never entered his head that his light could be obscured. But his British officer takes the indifference of the profane crowd to heart. When he hears the Sikh, Gurkha, and Pathan spoken of collectively as synonymous with the Indian Army he is displeased; and his displeasure is natural, if not philosophic. If he were philosophic he would find consolation in the same sheets which annoy him, for it is better to be ignored than to be advertised in a foolish way. It is with a joy that has no roots in pride that the Indian Army officer reads of the Gurkha hurling his kukri at the foe, or blooding his virgin blade on the forearms of the self-devoting ladies of Marseilles, or of the grave, bearded Sikhs handing round the hubble-bubble with the blood still wet on their swords; or of the Bengali lancer dismounting and charging the serried ranks of the Hun with his spear. Hearing of these wonders, the Sahib who commands the Punjabi Mussalman, and loves his men, will discover comfort in obscurity.

THE PATHAN

One often hears British officers in the Indian Army say that the Pathan has more in common with the Englishman than other sepoys. This is because he is an individualist. Personality has more play on the border, and the tribesman is not bound by the complicated ritual that lays so many restrictions on the Indian soldier. His life is more free. He is more direct and outspoken, not so suspicious or self-conscious. He is a gambler and a sportsman, and a bit of an adventurer, restless by nature, and always ready to take on a new thing. He has a good deal of *joie de vivre.* His sense of humour approximates to that of Thomas Atkins, and is much more subtle than the Gurkha's, though he laughs at the same things. He will smoke a pipe with the Dublin Fusiliers and share his biscuits with the man of Cardiff or Kent. He is a Highlander, and so, like the Gurkhas, naturally attracted by the Scot. Yet behind all these superficial points of resemblance he has a code which in ultimate things cuts him off from the British soldier with as clean a line of demarcation as an unbridged crevasse.

The Pathan's code is very simple and distinct in primal and essential things. The laws of hospitality, retaliation, and the sanctuary of his hearth to the guest or fugitive are seldom violated. But acting within the code the Pathan can indulge his bloodthirstiness, treachery, and vindictiveness to an extent unsanctioned by the tables of the law prescribed by other races and creeds. It is a savage code, and the only saving grace about the business is that the Pathan is true to it, such as it is, and expects to be dealt with by others as he deals by them. The main fact in life across the border is the badi, or blood-feud. Few families or tribes are without their vendettas. Everything that matters hinges on them, and if an old feud is settled by mediation through the Jirgah, there are seeds of a new one ready to spring up in every contact of life. The favour of women, insults, injuries, murder, debt, inheritance, boundaries, water-rights,—all these disputes are taken up by the kin of the men concerned, and it is a point of honour to assassinate,

To face p. 64.] THE PATHAN PIPERS.

openly or by stealth, any one connected by blood with the other side, however innocent he may be of the original provocation. Truces are arranged at times by mutual convenience for ploughing, sowing, or harvest; but as a rule it is very difficult for a man involved in a badi to leave his watch-tower, and still more difficult for him to return to it. It will be understood that the Pathan is an artist in taking cover. He probably has a communication trench of his own from his stronghold to his field, and no one better understands the uses of dead ground.

What makes these blood-feuds so endless and uncompromising is that quarrels begun in passion are continued in cold blood for good form. The Malik Din and Kambur Khil have been at war for nearly a century and nobody remembers how it all began. It is a point of honour to retaliate, however inconvenient the state of siege may be. The most ordinary routine of life may become impossible. The young Pathan may be itching to stroll out and lie on a bank and bask or fall asleep in the sun. But this would be to deliver himself into the hands of his enemy. There is no dishonour in creeping up and stabbing a man in the back when he is sleeping; but there is very great dishonour in failing to take an advantage of an adversary or neglecting to prosecute a blood feud to its finish. Such softness is a kind of moral leprosy in the eyes of the Pathan.

With so much at stake the Pathan cannot afford to be long away from home. In peace-time he frequently puts in for short leave. "Sahib," Sher Ali explains, "it is the most pressing matter." And the Sahib gathers that evil is likely to befall either Sher Ali's family or his neighbour Akbar Khan's during the next two weeks, and is bound by the brotherhood of arms to provide, so far as he is able, that it is not Sher Ali's. So the Pathan slips away from his regiment, anticipating the advertised date of his leave by consent, for there are men in his company connected by blood ties with the other party—men perhaps who are so far committed that they would lie up for Sher Ali themselves on a dark night if they were away on leave in their own country at the same time. But the code does not permit the prosecution of a vendetta in the regiment. A Pathan may find himself stretched beside his heart's abhorrence in a night picquet, the two of them alone together, alert, with finger on the trigger. They may have spent interminable long hours stalking each other in their own hills, but here they are safe as in sanctuary.

The trans-frontier Pathan would not wittingly have enlisted in the Indian Army if he could have foreseen the prospect of a three years' campaign in a foreign land. The security of his wife, his children, his cattle, his land, depend on his occasional appearance in his village. The interests of the Indian sepoy are protected by the magistrate and the police, but across the border the property of the man who goes away and fights may become the property of the man who stays at home. The exile is putting all the trump cards into his enemy's hands. The score will be mounting up against him. His name will become less, if not his kin; his womenkind may be dishonoured. In the event of his return the other party will have put up such a tally that it will take him all his time to pay off old scores. After a year of "the insane war" in which he has no real stake, and from which he can see no probable retreat, he is likely to take thought and brood. Government cannot protect his land and family; continued exile may mean the abandonment of all he has. In the tribal feud the man away on long service is likely to go under; the man on the spot has things all his own way.

Now the Pathan is a casuist. He is more strict in the observance of the letter of his code than in the observance of the spirit. An oath on the Koran is generally binding where there is no opening for equivocation, but it is not always respected if it can be evaded by a quibble. A Pathan informer was tempted by a police officer to give the names of a gang of dacoits.

"Sahib," he said, "I've sworn not to betray any son of man."

"You need not betray them," the officer suggested. "Don't tell me, tell the wall."

The Pathan was sorely tempted. He thought over the ethics. Then he smiled, and, like Pyramus, he addressed the wall:

"Oh! whited wall," he began, "their names are Mirza Yahya, Abdulla Khan . . ."

The code was not violated, as with a robust conscience the Pathan gave away the name of every man in the gang.

A tribesman who boasts that he would not injure a hair of an unclean swine which took sanctuary in his house, will conduct the guest with whom he has broken bread just beyond the limits of his property and shoot him. In a land dispute a mullah ordained that the two rival claimants should walk the boundary of the property in question on oath, each carrying a Koran on his head. They walked over the same ground, and each bore witness that he trod his paternal acres, and they did so without shame, for each had concealed a bit of his own undoubted soil in his shoe. When a round or two of ammunition are missing, the subadar of the company will raise a little heap of dust on the parade ground and make each man as he passes by plunge his clenched fist in it, and swear that he has not got the ammunition. The rounds are generally found in the dustheap, and nobody is perjured.

An officer in a Pathan militia regiment found a stumpy little tree stuck in the sand near the gate of the camp where trees do not grow. He was puzzled, and asked one Indian officer after another to explain. They all grinned rather sheepishly. "It is this way, Sahib," one of them said at last. "We lose a number of small things in the camp. Now when an object is lost the theft is announced, and each man as he passes the tree says, 'Allah curse the Budmash who stole the boots,' or the dish, or the turban, or whatever it may be. And so it will happen sometimes that the article will be found hanging in the fork of the tree in the morning when darkness gives place to light."

The Pathan cannot bear up under the weight of such commination, it spoils his sleep at night. Not that he has a sensitive conscience: theft, murder, and adultery are not crimes to him in the abstract, but only so far as they violate hospitality or loyalty to a bond. He has no sentiment, or inkling of chivalry; but he must save his face, avoid shame, follow the code, and prefer death to ridicule or dishonour. One of the axioms of his code is that he must be true to his salt. The trans-frontier Pathan is not a subject of the King as is the British Indian sepoy, but he has taken an oath. An oath is in the ordinary way binding, but if it can be shown that he has sworn unwittingly and against his religion—every text in the Koran is capable of a double interpretation—why, then the obligation is annulled. "Your religion comes first"—the argument is put to him by the Hun and the Turk. "No oath sworn to infidels can compel you to break your faith with Allah." The Pathan is not normally a religious fanatic any more than the Punjabi Mussalman. Had he been so he would not have ranged himself with us against an Islamic enemy, as he has done in every frontier campaign for the last half-century. But in this war Islam offered him the one decent retreat from an intolerable position.

There were one or two cases of desertion among the Pathans in France and Mesopotamia. The Pathan did not expect absolution if he fell into our hands afterwards, or if he were caught trying to slip away. Forgiveness is not in his nature. But think of the temptation, the easiness of self-persuasion. Remember how subtly the maggot of sophistry works even in the head of the Christian divine. Then listen to the burning words of the Jehad :—

"Act not so that the history of your family may be stained with the ink of disgrace and the blood of your Muhammadan brethren be shed for the attainment of the objects of unbelievers. We write this to you in compliance with the orders of God Almighty, the kind and also stern Avenger."

A hundred texts might be quoted, and have been quoted, from the Koran to show that it is obligatory for the Moslem soldier to fight against his King's enemies, whether they be of his own faith or no. But how many, after taking thought and counsel of expediency, are quite sure that black is not white after all! The deserter may not escape to the Hun lines and the pretended converts of Islam, whom instinct, stirring beneath the Jehadist's logic, must teach him to despise. And he is for the wall if he is caught, shamefully led out and bandaged and shot in the eyes of his brethren who have been true to their oath. None of us would hesitate to slip the trigger against a traitor of his kidney. The man's very memory is abhorred. Yet in dealing out summary execution one should remember the strong bias that deflected his mind. Out of the mud and poisoned gas of Flanders. Out of Mesopotamia. Out of the blood and fruitless sacrifice, the doom of celibacy, the monotony which is only broken by the variety it offers of different shapes of disease and death. Back to his tower and maize field if his kin have held them, and his wife if she has waited for him, and all in the name of honour and religion.

It may seem a mistake in writing of a brave people to take note of backsliders; but the instances in which the Pathan has been seduced from loyalty have been so discussed that it is better for the collective honour of the race to examine the psychological side of it frankly. It would be a great injustice to the Pathan if it were thought that any failed us through fear.

In courage and coolness the Pathan is the unquestioned equal of any man. Mir Dast, of Coke's Rifles F.F., attached to Wilde's Rifles F.F. in France, the first Indian officer to win the V.C., was a type of the best class of Afridi. No one who knew him was surprised to hear how, at the second battle of Ypres, after all his officers had fallen, he selected and consolidated a line with his small handful of men; how, though wounded and gassed himself, he held the ground he had hastily scratched up, walking fearlessly up and down encouraging his men; how, satisfied at last that the line was secure, he continued to carry in one disabled man after another, British and Indian, back to safety under heavy fire. Mir Dast had told the Colonel of the 55th, when he left the battalion in Bannu to join the regiment he was attached to in France, that he would not come back without the Victoria Cross. "Now that Indians may compete for this greatest of all bahadris," he said, "I shall return with it or remain on the field." And he did not say this in a boastful manner, but quietly as a matter of course, as though there were no other alternative; just as a boxer might tell you by way of assurance, repeating an understood thing, that he was going to fight on until the other man was knocked out. I met Mir Dast afterwards in hospital, and was struck with the extraordinary dignity and quiet reserve of the man; an impression of gallantry was conveyed in his brow and eyes, like a stamp on metal.

It was in the Mohmand compaign that Mir Dast won the I.O.M., in those days the nearest Indian equivalent to the V.C. An officer friend of mine and his who spoke to him in his stretcher after the fight, told me that he found Mir Dast beaming. "I am very pleased, Sahib," he said. "I've had a good fight, and I've killed the man that wounded me." And he held up his bayonet and pointed to a foot-long stain of blood. He had been shot through the thigh at three yards, but had lunged forward and got his man. On the same day another Afridi did a very Pathan-like thing. I will tell the story here, as it is typical of the impetuous, reckless daring of the breed, that sudden lust for honour which sweeps the Pathan off his feet, and carries him sometimes to the achievement of the impossible—an impulse, brilliant while it lasts, but not so admirable as the more enduring flame that is always trimmed and burns steadily without flaring.

Nur Baz was a younger man than Mir Dast, and one of the same Afridi company. It entered his head, just as it entered the head of Mir Dast when he left Bannu for France, that he must achieve something really remarkable. The young man was of the volatile, boastful sort, very different from the hero of Ypres, and to his quick imagination the conception of his bahadri was the same thing as the accomplishment of it, or the difference, if there were any, was only one of tense. So he began to talk about what he was going to do until he wearied the young officer to whom he was orderly. "Bring me your bahadri first, Nur Baz," the subaltern said a little impatiently, "then I shall congratulate you, but don't bukh so much about it."

The pride went out of Nur Baz at this snub as the air out of a pricked bladder, and he was very shamefaced until his opportunity came. This was in the same attack in which Mir Dast fell. The regiment were burning a village, and the Afridi company had to clear the ridge behind which commanded it; they and another Pathan company were attacking up parallel spurs. Nur Baz, finding that his orderly work committed him to a secondary *rôle* in the operations, asked if he might join his section, which was to lead the attack. He obtained his officer's consent, and was soon scrambling up the hillside in the pursuit. When the leading section extended he found the advance too slow, so he squatted behind a boulder, waited until the wave had got on a few yards, then dived down to the bottom of the nullah, climbed up again under cover, and in a few minutes appeared on the edge of the spur some 250 yards in advance of the assault. A yell of rage went up from the Pathans behind when they found that Nur Baz had forestalled them and was going to be first in at the death. But Nur Baz was happy as he leapt from one great boulder to another, the ground spitting up under him, and stopped every moment to get in a shot at the men in the sangar in front. Just as he reached it a Martini bullet struck his rifle in the small of the butt and broke off the stock. He could not fire now, but he fixed his bayonet and charged the sangar with his broken weapon. There were three men in it when he clambered over the parapet. One was dead, another who had missed him with his muzzle-loader a second or two before was reloading, and the third was slipping away. Nur Baz bayoneted the man who was reloading just as he withdrew the rod with which he was ramming the charge home; then he picked up the dead man's rifle and shot the fugitive; thus he cleared his little bit of front alone.

His subaltern had watched this very spectacular bit of bahadri from the parallel spur; but he only discovered that the central figure of it was his orderly when Mir Dast in his stretcher remarked, "Nur Baz has done well, Sahib, hasn't he?" Afterwards Nur Baz appeared "with a jaw like a bulldog, grinning all over, and the three rifles slung to his shoulder," and received the congratulations of his Sahib.

"Sahib," he said, "will you honour me by taking one of these? Choose the one you like best."

The subaltern selected the muzzle-loader, but Nur Baz demurred.

"I must first see the Colonel Sahib," he said, "if you choose that one."

"And why?"

"It is loaded, and it is not permitted to fire off a round in the camp without the Colonel Sahib's permission."

Just then the Colonel arrived, and Nur Baz, having obtained permission, raised the rifle jauntily to his shoulder and with evident satisfaction loosed the bullet which ought to have cracked his brain pan into the empty air. Nur Baz and Mir Dast, though differing much in style, both had a great deal of the original Pathan in them.

One more story of an Afridi. It was in France. There had been an unsuccessful attack on the German lines. A sergeant of the Black Watch was lying dead in no-man's land, and the Hun sniper who had accounted for him lay somewhere in his near neighbourhood; he had lain there for hours taking toll of all who exposed themselves. It was getting dark when an officer of the 57th Rifles saw a Pathan, Sher Khan, pushing his way along the trench towards the spot. The man was wasting no time; he was evidently on some errand, only he carried no rifle. The officer called after him:

"Hello, Sher Khan, where are you off to?"

"I am going to get the sniper, Sahib, who shot the sergeant."

"But why haven't you got a rifle?"

"I am not going to dirty mine, Sahib. I'll take the sergeant's."

It was still light when he crawled over the parapet and wriggled his way down a furrow to where the sergeant lay. The sniper saw him, and missed him twice. Sher Khan did not reply to this fire. He lay quite still by the side of the Highlander and gently detached one of his spats. This he arranged so that in the half light it looked like a white face peeping over the man's body. Then he withdrew twenty yards to one side and waited. Soon the Hun's head appeared from his pit a few yards off and disappeared quickly. But Sher Khan bided his time. The sniper was evidently intrigued, and as it grew darker he exposed himself a little more each time he raised his head peering at the white face over the dead Highlander's shoulder. At last he knelt upright, reassured—the thing was so motionless; nevertheless he decided that another bullet in it would do no harm. He was taking steady aim when the Pathan fired. The range was too close for a miss even in that light, and the Hun rolled over. Half an hour afterwards Sher Khan returned with the Hun's rifle and the Highlander's under his arm; in his right hand he carried the Hun's helmet, a grisly sight, as his bullet had crashed through the man's brain.

It is his individual touch, his brilliancy in initiative and coolness and daring in execution that has earned the Afridi his high reputation among Pathans. The trans-frontier Pathan with his eternal blood-feuds would naturally have the advantage in this kind of work over the Pathan from our side of the border; his whole life from his boyhood up is a preparation for it. That is why some of the most brilliant soldiers in the Indian Army have been Afridis. On the other hand, collectively and in companies, the cis-frontier Yusafzais and Khattaks have maintained a higher aggregate of the military virtues, especially in the matter of steadiness and "sticking it out."

A strange thing about the Pathan, and inconsistent with his hard-grained, practical nature, is that he is given to visions and epileptic fits. He is visited by the fairies, to use his own expressive phrase. I knew a fine old subadar who believed that these visitations came to him because he had shot a pigeon on a mosque. He became a prey to remorse, and made ineffectual pilgrimages to various shrines to exorcise the spirit. How much of this subconscious side of the Pathan is responsible for his state of mind when he runs amok would be an interesting point for the psychologist. The man broods over some injury or wrong and he is not content until he has translated his vision into fact. Sometimes he goes to work like the Malay, killing in a hot, blind fury. But there is often method in the orgy. It is an orgy of blood, one glorious hour, perhaps, or a few rapturous seconds in which vengeance is attained and satisfaction demanded of collective humanity, and the price to be paid for it, the Pathan's own life, is perfectly well understood.

Take the case of Ashgar Ali. He learnt that a disparaging report as to the work of his brother had been sent in to the O.C. of the battalion by one Fazal-ud-din, a non-commissioned Pathan officer. Fazal-ud-din slept with him in the same tent, and Ashgar Ali lay brooding and sleepless all night. Before day-break he had devised a plan. In the darkness he removed all the rifles from the tent and hid them outside. He waited till the moon rose.

Then standing by the door he shot the betrayer through the head as he slept. He shot another Pathan by his side who leapt to his feet, awakened by the report. Then he slipped away stealthily to the little round knoll which he had marked out for the catastrophe of his drama. Here he kept up a steady fire at any human shape that came within range, a stern dispenser of justice in full measure making good the errors of a too-biassed Providence. It was a calculated adjustment of right and wrong, and he kept a cool head as he counted up his tally. He saw his Colonel stalking him, an iron-grey head lifted cautiously from behind a hummock at fifty yards, an easy target. But Ashgar Ali called out, "Keep away, Sahib. I have no quarrel with you. My account is with the men. Keep away, or I must shoot." Snipers were firing at him at long range; a sepoy was creeping up behind, and almost as he spoke he rolled over and lay still.

A Pathan murder, as viewed by the assassin, generally stands for judgment and execution at the same time. There must be some such system among a people who have no Government or police. When a Pathan comes over the frontier and is arraigned by our code for a crime sanctioned by his own there is trouble. It is a tragic matter when law, especially if it is the Indian Penal Code, defeats the natural dispensations of justice. A splendid young Pathan, the pick of his battalion, was tried for shooting a man in his company. The act was deliberate, and to the Pathan mind justified by the provocation. The man who was put away meanly denied an obligation of honour. The Pathan shot him like a dog before a dozen witnesses, and no doubt felt the same generous thrill of satisfaction as he would have done in passing judgment in his own land. But to the disgust of the regiment, and more especially of the British officer, who understood the Pathan code, the upholder of honour, one of the best and straightest men they had, was hanged.

The great difference between the Pathan and the Sikh is that the Pathan is for himself. He has a certain amount of tribal, but no national, pride. His assurance is personal. Family pride depends on what the family has done within the memory of a generation; for there is little or no distinction in birth. The Pathan is genuinely a democrat, the Sikh only theoretically so. In strict accordance with his code the Sikh should be democratic, but whatever he may profess, he is aristocratic in spirit. His pride is in the community and in himself as one of the community. The prestige of the Khalsa is always in his mind. The Pathan's pride is there, but is latent. It leaps out quickly enough when challenged. But when the Pathan is boastful it is in a casual manner. Normally he does not bother his head about appearances. He is more like an Englishman in taking things as they come. But the Sikh is always acquisitive of honour. One cannot imagine Sikhs turning out old kit in order to save the new issue for handing in to the quartermaster when they "cut their name." Yet the Pathan, with his eye on the main chance, is quite content to go shabby if when he retires he can get more for his equipment on valuation. On one occasion on manœuvres, when a Pathan company had carried their economy in this respect a bit too far, their company commander got even with them in the kind of way they respect. Haversacks, water-bottles, coats, bandoliers, were laid on the ground for inspection. Then he sent them off to dig the perimeter. While they were digging some distance away, he went round quietly with an Indian officer and weeded out all the unserviceable kit. Then he sent for the men to come back. "I'm going to make a bonfire of these things," he said, "and what is more, you are going to dance round it." That young officer had the right way with the Pathan, who can enjoy a joke turned against himself better than most people. They danced round the fire, hugely amused, and no one resented it.

It must not be imagined that the Pathan is of a careful or saving disposition. He is out to enjoy himself, fond of all the good things of life, open-handed, and a born gambler. The money he would have saved on his new kit would probably have been gambled away a few days after he had "cut his name." I knew a regiment where some of the young Pathans on three and a half months' leave never went near their homes, but used to enlist in the coolie corps on the Bolan Pass simply for the fun of gambling! Gambling in the regiment, of course, was forbidden. But here they could have their fling and indulge a love of hazard. Wages were high and the place became a kind of tribal Monte Carlo. If they won, they threw up the work and had a good time; if they lost, it was all in the day's work.

The Pathan is very much a bird of passage in a regiment. He is a restless adventurer, and he is always thinking of "cutting his name." He likes a scrap on the frontier, but soldiering in peace-time bores him after a little while. It is all "farz kerna," an Orakzai said, "make believe," like a field-day. "You take up one position and then another, and nothing comes of it. One gets tired." Raids and rifle-thieving over the frontier are much better fun. The Pathan had the reputation of being the most successful rifle-thief we had rubbed up against in a campaign until we met the Arab in Mesopotamia. The Arab, when he goes about at night, seems to be leagued with Djinns; but in stealth, coolness, invisibility, daring, the Pathan runs him close. A sergeant of the Black Watch told me a characteristic story of how a Pathan made good a rifle he had lost in France. There had grown up a kind of *entente* between the Black Watch and Vaughan's Rifles, who held the line alongside of them. It could not be otherwise with two fighting regiments of like traditions who have advanced and retired together, held the same trenches and watched each other closely for months.

The Black Watch had been at Peshawar;

some of them could speak Hindustani, and one or two Pushtu. Their scout-sergeant, MacDonald, lost his rifle one night. He had stumbled with it into a ditch during a patrol, and left it caked with mud outside his dug-out when he turned in in the small hours. When he emerged it was gone, gathered in by the stretcher-bearers with the rifles of the dead and wounded, for MacDonald's dug-out was beside a first-aid station, and his rifle looked as if it belonged to a man who needed first aid.

He had to make a reconnaissance. There was a rumour that the enemy had taken down the barbed wire in the trenches opposite and were going to attack. It was the scout-sergeant's business to see. Luckily there was grass in no-man's-land knee-deep. But he wanted a rifle, and he turned to his good friends the Pathans as a matter of course.

"Ho, brothers!" he called out. "Where is the Pathan who cannot lay his hands on a rifle? I am in need of a rifle."

It was, of course, a point of honour with the 58th Rifles to deliver the goods. Shabaz Khan, a young Afridi spark, glided off in the direction from which the scout-sergeant had come.

MacDonald had not to wait many minutes before he returned with a rifle.

A few minutes afterwards he was slipping down the communication trench when he heard an oath and an exclamation behind him.

"By ——! There was eight rifles against the wall ten minutes ago, and now there's only seven, and nobody's been here."

It was the stretcher-bearer sergeant. MacDonald examined his rifle and found the regimental mark on the stock. He went on his way smiling. The Black Watch were brigaded with the 58th Rifles at Peshawar. "I remember," Sergeant MacDonald told me, "when the Highland Brigade Sports were held there, one of our fellows was tossing the caber—it took about six coolies to lift the thing. I thought it would impress the Pathans, but not a bit of it. I asked the old Subadar what he thought of MacAndrew's performance, and he said, 'It is not wonderful that you Jokes'—'Joke' was as near as he could get to Jock—'should do this thing. Are you not Highlanders (Paharis) like us, after all?'"

There is a marked difference in temperament among the Pathan tribes. The Mahsud is more wild and primitive than most, and more inclined to fanaticism. There are the makings of the Ghazi in him. On the other hand, his blood-feuds are more easily settled, as he is not so fastidious in questions of honour. The Afridi is more dour than the other, and more on his dignity. He has not the openness and cheerfulness of the Usafzai or Khattak, who have a great deal of the Celt in them. The Afridi likes to saunter about with a catapult or pellet bow. He will condescend to kill things, even starlings, but he does not take kindly to games. He is a good stalker and quite happy with a rifle or a horse. He excels in tent-pegging. But hockey and football do not appeal to him as much as they do to other sepoys, though he is no mean performer when he can be induced to play. This applies in a measure to all Pathans. An outsider may learn a good deal about their character by watching the way they play games. One cannot picture the Afridi, for instance, taking kindly to cricket, but a company of them used to get some amusement out of net practice in a certain frontier regiment not long ago. An officer explained the theory of the game. The bat and ball did not impress the Pathan, but the gloves and pads pleased his eye with their suggestion of defence.

Directly the elements of a man-to-man duel were recognized cricket became popular. They were out to hurt one another. They did not care to bat, they said, but wished to bowl, or rather shy. The Pathan likes throwing things, so he was allowed to shy. Needless to say the batsman was the mark and not the wicket. A good, low, stinging drive to the off got one of the men on the ankle. Shouts of applause. First blood to the Sahib. But soon it is the Pathan's turn to score. His quick eye designs a stratagem in attack. By tearing about the field he has collected three balls, and delivers them in rapid succession standing at the wicket. The first, a low full-pitch, goes out of the field; the second, aimed at the Sahib's knee, is neatly put into the slips, but the batsman has no time to guard the third, hurled with great violence at the same spot, and it is only the top of his pad that saves him from the casualty list.

The Pathan is more careless and happy-go-lucky than the Punjabi Mussalman, and not so amenable to discipline. It is his jaunty, careless, sporting attitude, his readiness to take on any new thing, that attracts the British soldier. That rifle-thief of the 58th was dear to Sergeant

MacDonald. But it is difficult to generalize about the Pathan as a class. There is a sensible gulf fixed between the Khattak and the Afridi, and between the Afridi and the Mahsud. I think, if it were put to the vote among British officers in the Indian Army, the Khattak would be elected the pick of the crowd. A special chapter is devoted to him in this volume, and as his peculiar virtues are discoverable in some degree among other classes of Pathans, the Khattak chapter may be regarded as a continuation of the present one. There used to be an idea that the cis-frontier Pathan, by reason of his settled life and the security of the policeman and the magistrate round the corner, was not a match for the trans-frontier Pathan who adjusted his own differences at the end of a rifle. But the war has proved these generalizations unsafe. The Pathan is a hard man to beat whichever side of the border he hails from; but in a war like this he is all the better for being born a subject of the King.

THE DOGRA

CHANCE threw me among the Dogras after a battle, and I learnt more of these north-country Rajputs than I had ever done in times of peace. Everybody knows how they left Rajputana before the Muhammadans conquered the country and so never bowed to the yoke, how they fought their way north, cut out their own little kingdoms, and have held the land they gained centuries ago by the sword. I have travelled in the foothills where they live, both in Kangra and Jammu, and can appreciate what they owe to a proud origin and a poor soil. But one cannot hope to learn much of a people in a casual trek through their country. The Dogra is shy and does not unbosom himself to the stranger. Even with his British officer he is reserved, and one has to be a year or more with him in the regiment before he will talk freely of himself. But the confidence of the British officer in the Dogra is complete, and his affection for him equals that of the Gurkha officer for "the

To face p. 92.] THE DOGRA.

Gurkha." "He is such a Sahib," the subaltern explained. "You won't find another class of sepoy in the Indian army who is quite such a Sahib as the Dogra."

And here I must explain that I am only setting down what the subaltern told me, that I tapped him on the subject he loved best, and that I am making no invidious comparisons of my own. One seldom meets a good regimental officer who does not modify one's relative estimate of the different fighting stocks of the Indian Army. Still one can discriminate. What the subaltern told me about the gallantry of the Dogras I saw afterwards repeated in "Orders" by the General of the Division. There were other regiments which received the same praise, and if I had fallen among these I should have heard the same tale.

"The first thing we knew of that trench," the subaltern explained, "was when the Turkey-cock blazed off into us at three hundred yards. Thank heaven, our fellows were advance guard."

I smiled at the boy's delightful conceit in his own men. His company were sitting or lying down on the banks of a water-cut in the restful attitudes men fall into after strain. They were most of them young men, clean-shaven with neat moustaches, lightly built but compact and supple, of regular features, cast very much in a type. Some were smoking their chillums, the detached bowl of a huqah, which they hold in their two palms and draw in the smoke between the fingers through the aperture at the base. The Dogra is an inveterate smoker and will have his chillum out for a final puff two minutes before going into the attack. I was struck by their scrupulous neatness. The morning had been the third day of a battle. The enemy had decamped at dawn, but in the two previous days half the regiment had fallen. Yet they seemed to have put in a toilet somehow. Their turbans, low in the crown with the shell-like twist in front peculiar to the Dogra, were as spick and span as on parade. They looked a cool crowd, and it was of their coolness under the most terrible fire that the subaltern spoke. One of them was readjusting his pagri by a mirror improvised out of a tin he had picked up in the mud, and was tying it in neat folds.

"The Dogra is a bit fussy about his personal appearance," the subaltern explained. "He is a blood in his way. I have seen our fellows giving their turbans the correct twist when they are up to the neck in it during an advance.

"It was the devil of a position. The Turkey-cock lay doggo and held his fire. We didn't see a sign of him until he popped off at us at three hundred yards. Their trenches had no parapets and were almost flush with the ground. In places they had built in ammunition boxes which they had loopholed and plastered over with mud. They had dotted the ground in front with little mounds which they used as range-marks, and they had every small depression which offered any shelter covered with their machine-guns."

And he told me how the Dogras pressed on to the attack over this ground with a shout—not the "Ram Chandra ji ki jai" of route marches and manœuvres, but with a "Ha, aha, aha, aha, aha," a sound terrifying in volume, and probably the most breath-saving war cry there is.

A great many of the regiment were new to the game, mere boys of seventeen, and the old hands had piqued their vanity, reminding them that they had never been in battle and expressing a pious hope that they would stand their ground. The subaltern had to pull some of these striplings down who exposed themselves too recklessly.

He pointed out to me one Teku Singh, "a top-hole fellow." In the trench a machine-gun jammed, Teku Singh clambered out to adjust it. The subaltern called to him to keep his head down. "What does dying matter, Sahib?" he answered, echoing at Sheikh Saad the spirit of Chitore. "The only fit place for a Rajput to die is on the field of battle." Teku Singh was modestly smoking his chillum on the bund.

The Dogra's is an unobtrusive gallantry. He is no thruster. He has not the Pathan's devil-may-care air, nor the Sikh's pleasing swagger. When a group of Indian officers are being introduced to an inspecting general or the ruler of a province, you will find it is the Dogra who hangs in the background. Yet he is intensely proud, conservative, aristocratic. The subaltern's description of Teku Singh at home reminded me of the hero of the "Bride of Lammermuir," that classic and lovable example of the impoverished aristocrat, whose material poverty is balanced by more honourable possessions. I have seen the land the Dogra cultivates. It is mostly retrieved from a stony wilderness. His cornfields are often mere sockets in the rock over which a thin layer of earth has gathered.

His family traditions forbid him to work on the soil and compel him to keep a servant, though he has been known to plough secretly by night. Under-fed at home, he will not accept service save in the army. There are families who do nothing but soldiering. There is no difficulty about recruits. "When a man goes home on leave," the subaltern explained, "he brings back his pals. There is always a huge list of umedwars (candidates) to choose from. It is like waiting to get into the Travellers or the Senior Naval and Military."

Most of the men in the regiment were Katoch Dogras from the Kangra district, the most fastidious of all. They won't plough, and won't eat unless their food is cooked by a Katoch or a Brahmin. There are families who will only join the cavalry. The plough they disdain, as they boast that the only true weapon of a Rajput is the sword; when driven by hunger and poverty to cultivate their land themselves, they do it secretly, taking out their oxen by night and returning before daylight. The head of the house has his talwar, or curved Indian sword with a two-and-a-half-foot blade. It is passed down as an heirloom from father to son, and is

H

carried on campaigns by the Dogra officer. I have seen them in camp here, though they are not worn in the trenches. The Dogra has a splendid heart, but his physique is often weakened by poverty. It is extraordinary how they fill out when they come into the regiment. It is the same, of course, with other sepoys, but there is more difference between the Dogra recruit and the seasoned man than in any other stock. The habit of thrift is so ingrained in them that it is difficult to prevent them stinting themselves in the regiment. The subaltern had a story of a recruit who left his rations behind on manœuvres. It was the General himself who discovered the delinquent. Asked for an explanation the lad thought awhile and then answered bashfully, "Sahib, when I am fighting I do not require food."

Every Dogra is shy and reserved and very sensitive about his private affairs. When his name is entered in the regimental sheet roll, the young recruit is asked who is his next of kin.

"Wife," he will say bashfully.

"What age?"

He is not quite certain, thinks she is about twelve.

"How high is she?"

"About so high." He stretches his hand four feet from the ground.

He is dreadfully bashful as he makes this gesture, afraid the other recruits should hear, just like a boy in the fourth form asked to describe his sister's complexion or hair.

Needless to say, the Dogra seldom, if ever, brings his wife into cantonments. Exile must be harder to him than to many as he is the most home-loving person. His only crime is that when he goes to his village he sometimes runs things too close, so that an accident by the way, a broken wheel or swollen stream, makes him overstay his leave.

"I wish I could show you Moti Chand," the subaltern continued. "He was a mere boy not turned seventeen. This show was the first time he had been under fire; he was one of the ammunition-carriers and had to go from the front trenches to the first-line transport and bring back his box. He made two journeys walking slowly and deliberately as they all do, very erect, balancing the ammunition-box on his head. When he came up the second time I told him to hurry up and get down into the trenches.

'No, Sahib,' he said, 'Ram Chand, who was coming up beside me, was killed. I must go back and bring in his box.' He brought in the box all right, but was shot in the jaw. I think he is doing well.

"I can tell you, you would like the Dogra if you knew him. He is difficult to know and his reserve might make you think him sulky at first, but there is nothing sulky or brooding about him. He never bears a grudge; he is rather a cheery fellow and has his own sense of humour. As a shikari——"

The subaltern sang the praises of Teku Singh and Moti-Chand in a way which was very pleasant to hear. He told me how their families received him in Kangra, every household insisting that he should drink tea, and he ended up by repeating that the true Dogra was the most perfect sahib he knew.

It was no new experience for me to hear the Dogra praised. Their fighting qualities are well known, and they have proved themselves in many a frontier campaign, more especially in the capture of Nilt (1891), and in the defence of Chitral and in the memorable march to the relief of the garrison. And one had heard of the

Dogra officer, Jemadar Kapur Singh, in France, who held on until all but one wounded man had been put out of action, and then rather than surrender shot himself with his last cartridge. Besides the three Dogra class regiments, the 37th, 38th, and 41st, there are many Dogra companies in mixed-company battalions, and Dogra squadrons in cavalry regiments. They may not make up a large part of the Indian Army, but they contribute a much larger part in proportion to their numbers than any other stock.

When next I met the subaltern the regiment had been in action again and he had been slightly wounded. He took me into his tent and showed me with pride what the General had written about his Dogras. One of them, Lance-Naik Lala, had been recommended for the Victoria Cross; he was the second sepoy in Mesopotamia on whom the honour was conferred.

"You'll see I haven't been talking through my hat," he explained. "Lala was at it all day and most of the night, and earned his V.C. a dozen times. It seemed certain death to go out to ——; the enemy were only a hundred yards off."

"Lance-Naik Lala insisted on going out to

his Adjutant," the recommendation ran, "and offered to crawl back with him on his back at once. When this was not permitted, he stripped off his own clothing to keep the wounded officer warmer, and stayed with him till just before dark when he returned to the shelter. After dark he carried the first wounded officer back to the main trenches, and then, returning with a stretcher, carried back his Adjutant."

This was at El Hannah on the 21st January. There was a freezing wind and the wounded lay out in pools of rain and flooded marsh all night; some were drowned; others died of exposure. It was a Dogra-like act of Lala to strip himself, and to make a shield of his body for his Adjutant, an act of devotion often repeated by the sepoy in Mesopotamia; and the Adjutant was only one of five officers and comrades whom Lala saved that day.

In a special issue of orders the Divisional General spoke of the splendid gallantry of the 41st Dogras in aiding the Black Watch to storm and occupy the enemy's trenches. The 6th Jats and 97th Infantry were mentioned with the Dogras. Of the collective achievement of the four regiments on that day the General wrote:—

"Their advance had to be made across a perfectly open, bullet-swept area, against sunken loop-holed trenches in broad daylight, and their noble achievement is one of the highest. The great and most admirable gallantry of all ranks, and especially that of the British officers, is worthy of the highest commendation. They showed the highest qualities of endurance and courage under circumstances so adverse as to be almost phenomenal."

THE MAHRATTA

I SAW it stated in a newspaper that one of the surprises of the war has been the Mahratta. "Surprise" is hardly a tactful word; and it points back to a time when two or three classes of sepoy were praised indiscriminately to the disparagement of others. The war has brought about a readjustment of values. Not that the more tried and proven types have disappointed expectation; the surprise is that less conspicuous types have made good.

In France one heard a great deal about the Garhwali; in Mesopotamia the Cinderella of the Indian Army was undoubtedly the Mahratta.

That his emergence should be a surprise was illogical. The Mahratta horseman was once a name to conjure with, and the sword of Siwoji has left a dint in history legible enough. He was once the "Malbrovck" of Hindustan. If the modern Mahratta has fallen under an eclipse the cause has been largely geographical. Our

To face p. 104.] THE KONKANI MAHRATTA.

frontier campaigns have never offered the Indian Army active service enough to go round; certainly the Bombay Army has not come in for its share, and Saihan, on the 15th of November, 1914, was the first pitched battle in which a Mahratta regiment, constituted as such, had been engaged. What honour he earned before that went to swell the collective prestige of class-company regiments; for it was not until the Indian Army was reorganised in 1897 that the Mahratta battalion came into being. The British officer, of course, in these regiments knew his sepoy; he believed that the Dekkan and Konkan produced as stout a breed as any other soil, and he would tell you so in the most definite terms, and remind you how the Mahrattas proved their mettle at Maiwand. But then one never listened seriously to a regimental officer when he talked about his own men.

The Sapper in a field company with divers races under his command is listened to with less suspicion. It was a Sapper who first opened my eyes to the virtue of a Mahratta, and that was before the war.

"Who do you think the pick of your lot?" I asked.

"The Mahratta," he replied, unhesitatingly.

"Because he can dig?"

"None better. But it is his grit I was thinking of. I'd as soon have a Mahratta with me in a scrap as any one."

One heard little or nothing of the Mahratta in France. Yet it was a Mahratta who earned the Médaille Militaire—I believe the first bestowed on an Indian—for an unobtrusive bit of work at Givenchy on the 11th of December, 1914. We took a German saphead that day and drove the Huns down their communication trench, and then we had to sap back to our own lines, while another sap was being driven forward to meet us. For twenty-three hours the small party was cut off from the rest of the lines, and they worked steadily with their backs to the enemy, bombed at and fired on the whole time. Supplies and ammunition ran short, and we threw them a rope with a stone on it, and they dragged ammunition and food and bombs into the trench, bumping over the German dead, and the Mahratta took his turn at the traverse covering the party, as cool as a Scot.

There were but a sprinkling of them in Flanders, a few Sappers and Miners and two companies of the 107th Pioneers. It was left to Force "D" to discover that the Mahratta has as big a heart for his size as any sepoy in the Indian Army. To follow the exploits of the Mahratta battalions from the battle of Saihan on the 15th November, 1914, to Ctesiphon is to follow the glorious history of the 6th Division. Up to and including Ctesiphon, no Mahratta battalion was given a position to attack which it did not take, and in the retirement on Kut-el-Amarah their steadiness was well proved. It is a record which is shared with other regiments; but this chapter is concerned with the Mahratta alone. They were in nearly every fight, and for a long time they made up a fourth part of the whole force.

It was the 117th who, with the Dorsets, took the wood, and cleared the Turks out of their trenches at Saihan. It was the 110th, with the Norfolks, who led the attack on Mazeera village on the 4th December, clearing the left bank of the river; and a double company of the regiment captured the north face of the Qurnah position four days afterwards. Two battalions of the Mahrattas were in the front line again at Shaiba when the Turks were routed in one of the hardest fought and most critical battles of the campaign. They were at Nasiriyeh and Amara, and they were a tower of strength in the action at Sinn which gave us Kut-el-Amarah. Here all three battalions—the 103rd, 110th, and 117th—were engaged. They went without water and fought three consecutive engagements in forty-eight hours. The 117th, with the Dorsets, and the 22nd company of Sappers and Miners, were the first troops to enter the enemy's trenches. They broke through the wire and rushed the big redoubt, led by a subadar-major when all their British officers had fallen. At Ctesiphon again they covered themselves with glory. The British regiment brigaded with them speak well of these hard-bitten men, and many a villager of Dorset, Norfolk, or Oxford will remember the Mahratta, and think of him as a person one can trust.

"What was the Indian regiment on your right?" I heard a Norfolk man ask another, in discussing some obscure action on the Tigris of a year ago.

"The —— Mahrattas."

The Bungay man nodded. "Ah, they wouldn't leave you up a tree."

"Not likely."

And being familiar with the speech of Norfolk men, who are sparing of tribute, or admiration, or surprise, I knew that the "Mahratta" had received a better "chit" than even the Sapper had given him.

It was in the trenches, and I had been getting the Norfolks to tell me about the thrust up the river in the winter of 1914.

There was a lull in the firing. The Turks, 200 yards ahead, were screened from us by the parapet; and as I stood with my back to this looking eastward, there was nothing visible but earth and sky and the Norfolk men, and a patch of untrodden field, like a neglected lawn, running up to the next earth-work, and yellow with a kind of wild mustard. The flowers and grasses and a small yellow trefoil, wild barley, dwarf mallow, and shepherd's purse were Norfolk flowers. They and the broad, familiar accent of the men made the place a little plot of Norfolk. Nothing Mesopotamian impinged on the homeliness of the scene.

And beyond the traverse were the Mahrattas, sons of another soil. They were a new draft, most of them mere boys who had come straight from the plough into this hard school. They looked dreamy and pensive, with a not very intelligent wistfulness, but they were ready for anything that was going on. Two of them were sniping from a loophole. One of them was shot in the shoulder through a sandbag while I was there. Soon after dark I saw a batch of six with an officer step over the parapet into that particularly horrid zone called no-man's-land. They were to look for surface mines and to be careful not to tread on one. The bullets cracked against the parapet, but they were as casual as if they were going out to pick mushrooms.

The "mines" were charged shell-cases lying flat on the ground. The difficulty with these young recruits was to prevent them feeling for them with their feet or prodding them with a bayonet. They were quite untrained, but there was the same stuff in them as in the men who fought at Shaiba and Ctesiphon, and boasted that they had never been beaten by the Turks. A boy of seventeen who had gone out a few nights before was shot in the leg and lost his patrol. In the morning he found he was crawling up to the Turkish trenches. He was out all that day, but got back to his regiment at night, and all the while he hung on to his rifle.

The Subaltern had been a little depressed with this new batch of recruits. There was so little time to knock them into shape, and he was particularly pleased that Ghopade had brought back his rifle.

"They've got the right spirit," he said. "It's only a question of a month or two. But look at these children."

They certainly did not look very smart or alert or particularly robust.

"This one doesn't look as if he could stick a Turk," I said, and pointed to a thin hatchet-faced lad who could not have weighed much more than eight stone.

"Oh, I expect he'd do that all right. They are much wirier than you would think. It's their turn-out I mean."

"They've been in the trenches a week," I said, by way of extenuation. But the Subaltern and I had passed by the —th and the —th in the same brigade, equally trench-bound, and they were comparatively spick and span.

The Mahratta sepoy is certainly no swash-buckler. To look at him, with his dark skin and irregular features, you would not take him for a member of a military caste. No one cares less for appearance; and his native dress—the big, flat pagri, dhoti, and large loose shoes of the Dekkan and Konkan—do not lend themselves to smartness. Nor does the King's uniform bring with it an immediate transformation. The unaccustomed military turban, which the Sikh or Pathan ties deftly as if with one fold, falls about the head and down the neck of the Mahratta in the most capricious convolutions. If he is a Bayard he does not look the part, and looks, no doubt, as well as his geographical position, have stood in the way of his finding himself. Anyhow, the men who move the pawns on the board in the war-game had long passed him over.

The Mahratta battalions are not, strictly speaking, class regiments, for they each contain a double company of Dekkan Muhammadans. These, but for their inherited religion, are not very widely separated from the Mahrattas. They too have brought honour to the Dekkan. At Ctesiphon a double company of them were attacking a position. They lost all five officers, the British subaltern killed, two jemadars wounded, two subadars killed. One subadar, Mirza Rustum Beg, was wounded twice in the attack, but went

THE DEKHANI MUSSALMAN.

To face p. [12.]

on and received his death-wound within twenty-five yards of the enemy. The rest of the company went on, led by the havildars, and took the trench at the point of the bayonet.

That is not a bad record for a class of sepoy who has probably never been mentioned in the newspapers during the war. But it has been a war of "surprises," and one of the morals of Mesopotamia is that one ought not to be surprised at anything. What the Mahratta and Dekkani Muhammadan have done may be expected from—has, indeed, been paralleled by—other hardened stocks. With good leading and discipline and the moral that tradition inspires, you can make good troops out of the agriculturist in most lands, provided he is not softened by a too yielding soil.

The Mahratta has no very marked characteristics to distinguish him from other sepoys. He is just the bedrock type of the Indian cultivator, the real backbone of the country. And he has all the virtues and limitations which you will find in the agriculturist whether he be Sikh, Rajput, Dogra, Jat, or Mussalman, whether he tills the land in the Dekkan or Peshawar. A prey to the priests, money-lenders and vakils, litigious, slow-thinking, unsophisticated—but of strong affections, long-enduring and brave. The small landowner, where the soil resists him and the elements chastise, is much the same all over the world.

THE JAT

THE Jat, as we have seen, is the backbone of the Punjab; for it is from this Scythian breed that most of the Sikhs and a number of the Punjabi Mussalmans derive their sinews and stout-heartedness. If you used the word in its broad ethnic sense, signifying all classes of Jat descent, the muster would include the best part of the roll of modern Indian chivalry. But it is with the Hindu Jat, whose ancestors were not seduced or intimidated by Islam and who himself is not sufficiently attracted by the Khalsa to become a Sikh, that this chapter deals. That neither material expediency, love of honour, nor the glamour of an ideal has turned him aside from the immemorial path of his ancestors presupposes a certain stolidity, in which one is not disappointed when one knows the man.

I have passed many years in a district where there are Jats, but the Jat villager is not the same man as the Jat sepoy, and I did not make acquaintance with the sepoy breed until I ran across the bomb-havildar of the 6th Jats in Mesopotamia.

I was taking my bully, and "Tigris" and whisky, with a Jat regiment, the 6th, when the discussion arose as to why the Jat wears gold in his teeth. The doctor thought the idea was that gold carried you over the Styx; it was a kind of Elysian toll. I persuaded the Colonel to call one of the men into the dug-out and to draw him on the point. So Tara, the bomb-havildar, was sent for, a jiwan of five years' service and the quickest intelligence in the regiment.

Tara entered, saluted and stood at attention, each joint of him independently stiff and inflexible, the stiffest wooden soldier could not be more stiff than he, and his rifle was speckless in spite of the mud. At the O.C.'s command his limbs became more independent of one another, but rigidity was still the prominent note.

"Why do Jats wear gold in their teeth, Tara?" the Colonel asked: "this Sahib wants to know."

Tara pondered.

To face p. 116.] A JAT CAMEL SOWAR.

"For the sake of appearance, Sahib," he said, "to give them an air."

"Is there no other reason?"

Tara consulted the tarpaulin overhead, the mud walls, the mud table of the mess, where "La Vie Parisienne" and a Christmas annual gave the only bit of relief to this dun-coloured habitation. Then he smiled and delivered himself slowly, "There is a saying among my people, Sahib, that he who wears gold in his teeth must always speak what is true. Gold in the teeth stops the passage of lies."

"But you have no gold in your teeth?"

"No, Sahib."

"Is that why you tell the tall story about all those Germans you killed at Festubert?"

Tara smiled at this thrust.

"No, Sahib," he said, laughing. "It is true I killed ten between two traverses."

"Better ask him right out, sir," the doctor suggested.

"I have heard some story about gold helping the Jat to heaven," the Colonel observed to Tara.

The gleam of reminiscence in the havildar's eyes, as he confirmed this legend, showed that he was not speaking merely to please. It was the old story of Charon. Gold, he explained, was a passport in the other world as in this, and it was not safe to carry it on the finger or on the ear where it might be detached, so it was worn in the teeth.

"And who puts it there?"

"The goldsmith, Sahib," and he enlarged upon the exorbitance of the Sonari; for the Jat is as thrifty as the Scot.

It was on account of these charges that Tara had omitted the rite.

"When you go back to your village," the Colonel said, dismissing him, "don't forget to visit the Sonari, and then you will not tell any more lies."

Tara saluted with an irradiating smile.

"Assuredly, Sahib, I will not forget," he said. "I shall go straight to the Sonari."

This was quite a sally for Tara, and we all laughed, for the Jat is not quick at repartee. The way we had to dig the story out of him was characteristic, but he is not as a rule so responsive to badinage. The Jat has no time for play. When he is a boy he is too busy looking after the cows, and his nose is kept at the grindstone until he crumbles into the soil that bore him. He has no badges, flags, emblems, no peculiar way of tying his turban or wearing his clothes; and he has very little sentiment. It was a stroke of genius in Guru Gobind Singh when he turned the Jat into a Sikh, gave him the five badges, and wedded him to steel. Tradition grew with the title of Singh, and a great military brotherhood was founded: but in the unconverted Jat there is the same strong fibre, the stronger, the regimental officer will tell you, for not having been uprooted or pruned, and he prides himself that he will make as good a soldier out of the Jat as ever the Guru did.

The Jat is primarily a farmer. He has not the ancient military traditions of the Rajput, Mahratta, or Sikh, though none so stubborn as he to fight for his own land. He does not figure in history among the adventurers, builders of kingdoms, leaders of men, but circumstance has moulded him from time to time into a fighting man. Prosperity may soften him, but adversity only stiffens the impression of the mould.

It was during the reconstitution of the Indian Army in 1893, that the Jats were built up again into a fighting race. A good regimental officer can make anything he will out of the Jat. It takes earthquakes and volcanoes to turn a regiment of these hard-bitten men out of a position they have been given to hold. If the Jat is wanting in initiative and enterprise, this is merely a defect of a virtue, for once set going it never enters his honest hard head to do anything else but go on. And that is why the Jat has done so well in this war. Every knock hardens him. Courage is often the outcome of ignorance, but the remnants of a Jat battalion which has been wiped out half a dozen times will go into the attack again as unconcerned as a new draft.

The 6th Jats was one of the first of the Indian regiments to be engaged in France. As early as the 16th of November, 1914, they had broken into the German trenches. It was on the 23rd of the same month that they made the gallant counter-attack over the snow at Festubert with the Garhwalis and won back the lost trenches. At Givenchy, on December 20th, they held their ground against the German wave when they were left practically in the air; and they would not let go their hold at Neuve-

Chapelle when they were enfiladed from the Port Arthur position, still intact, on their right. Two months afterwards, on the 9th of May, they made their frontal attack on Port Arthur. A double company penetrated the German lines; only seven men returned unwounded. History repeated itself in Mesopotamia. It has been the part of this gallant stock to arrive on the scene in the nick of time and to be thrown into the brunt of the attack.

The Jat is not troubled with nerves or imagination, and he is seemingly unacquainted with fear. Alarums, bombardments, and excursions having become his normal walk of life, he will continue on his path, probably with fewer inward questionings than most folk, until the end of the war. Give him a trench to hold and he will stick to it as a matter of course until he is ordered to come out.

The regiment in the trenches were mostly Jats of Hissar and Rohtak, and the Colonel told me with the pride that is right and natural in the regimental officer that this was the best stock. "You must get the Jat where he is top dog in his own country," he said, "and not where he lives among folk who think they are his betters.

And he is best where the land is poor. In districts where the sub-division of the soil among large families does not leave enough to go round you will get a good recruit." Locality is all important; a dividing river may make all the difference. The Colonel admired the Jats of A, but he had no good word for the Jats of B. The Rajput Jat, especially from Bikaner, he admitted, were stout fellows, though they were not of his crew. There were well-to-do districts in which the Jat would not follow the pursuit of arms whether in peace or in war. "And if you want recruits," he enjoined on me, "don't go to an irrigated district." Water demoralises them. When a Jat sits down and watches the canal water and the sun raise his crop, his fibre slackens, for his stubborn qualities proceed from the soil. It is the same with other agricultural classes in the Indian Army, but the Jat is probably the best living advertisement of the uses of adversity. There is a proverb in the Punjab on the lines of our own tag about the three things that are most improved by flagellation, but woman is the only item recommended in both cases. The Hindu variant adds "flax" and "the Jat."

There is another rude proverb of the country. "Like Jat, like byle (ox)." There are many Jats and most of them have some peculiar virtue of their own, but quickness of apprehension is not one of them. I had an amusing reminder of this before I left the trench. Bullets were spattering against the parapet with a crack as loud as the report of a rifle, and our own and the Turkish shells screamed over the dug-out with so confused a din that one was never quite sure which was which. It was the beginning of the afternoon "strafe." Still there was no call for casualties, and one only had to keep one's head low. In the middle of it a subaltern coming down "Queen Street" looked in and told us that one of the Jats was hit. "Loophole?" the Colonel asked. But it was not a loophole. The jiwan had got hold of somebody's periscope; he had heard that it was a charm which enables you to see without being hit—he was standing up over the parapet trying to adjust it like a pair of field glasses, when a bullet flicked off part of his ear.

The supply of good Indian officers is sometimes a difficulty in a Jat regiment, for these children of labour follow better than they lead.

But even in the acquisition of understanding it is hard plugging application that tells. "Continuing" is the Jat's virtue, or "carrying on" as we say, and he will sap through a course of signalling with the same doggedness as he saps up to the enemy's lines. "We've got some first class signallers," the Colonel boasted, "they can write their reports in Roman Urdu."

And the pick of the lot was Tara. What that youth has seen in France and Mesopotamia would keep old Homer in copy through a dozen Iliads, but it has left no wrinkle on his brow. Tara is still as fresh as paint.

"Sahib," he asks, "when may I go to the Turkish saphead with my bombs?" He lost a brother at Sheikh Saad and wants to make good.

THE RAJPUT AND BRAHMAN

In the early days before the British Raj had spread North and West, there was a period when the Bengal Army was enlisted almost exclusively from the high-caste Hindu. In the campaigns against the Muhammadan princes the Mussalman sepoy, for reasons of expediency, was gradually weeded out. The Gurkha was unknown to Clive's officers; the day of the Sikh and Mahratta was not yet; the Dogra was undiscovered; there was a sprinkling of Pathan adventurers in the ranks and a few Jats and Rohillas; but, generally speaking, the Rajput and Brahman had something like a monopoly in military service.

The Rajputs, of course, are *par excellence* the military caste of Hindustan, and there is no more glorious page in the annals of chivalry than the story of that resistance to the successive waves of Moslem invaders. Three times the flower of the race were annihilated in the defence of Chitore. But they never yielded, for the Rajput would take no quarter. He was true to his oath not to yield; and when the odds against him offered no hope of victory, his only care was to sell his life dearly and to cut his way deep into the ranks of the enemy before he fell. The women, too, refused the dishonour of survival. Led by their queen and the princesses they passed into a sepulchre of flame. Others fought and fell beside their husbands and sons, and their courage was celebrated by the pen of Akbar, whose testimony to the spirit of the race does not fall short of the Rajput bards.

The Rajput of to-day does not hold the same pre-eminence in the army as did his ancestors. His survival in the land he held so bravely is due to the British, who only came in time to save the race, exhausted by centuries of strife, from conquest by more vigorous invaders. Yet it was on the Rajput and the Brahman more than on any other class of sepoy that we depended in our early campaigns. They fought with us against the French; they helped us to crush the Nawab of Oudh. They served with conspicuous gallantry in the Mahratta, Nepal,

To face p. 126.] THE RAJPUT.

Afghan, and Sikh wars. They formed part of the gallant band that defended the Residency at Lucknow.* And later in Egypt, Afghanistan, and Burma, they maintained the honour they had won. Had there been class regiments in those days the izzat of the Rajput and Brahman sepoy would have been higher than it is.

The Brahmans only enlist in two class regiments of the Indian Army. The type recruited is of magnificent physique; their breeding and pride of race is reflected in their cleanliness and smartness on parade. They are fine athletes, expert wrestlers, and excel in feats of strength; and they have a high reputation for courage. Unhappily they have seen little service since the class system was introduced, and so have not had the opportunity of adding to a distinguished record.

For various reasons the Rajput does not enlist so freely in the Indian Army as his proud military traditions might lead one to expect. The difficulties of recruiting are greatest among the classes which should provide the best material. The difference of quality among

* The remnants of "the gallant few" became the nucleus of the Loyal 16th Regiment.

Rajput sepoys is to a large extent determined by the locality of enlistment. Those from Rajputana and the neighbouring districts of the Punjab as a rule rank higher than recruits from the United Provinces and Oudh. The western Rajputs, generally of purer blood, are not so fastidious about caste, while farther east, especially Benares way, the Rajput is inclined to become Brahmanised. Brahmanism, whatever its merits, is not a good forcing ground for the military spirit. Exclusiveness is the bane of "the twice-born," especially in war. On service the essentials of caste are observed among Rajputs and Brahmans as fastidiously as in peace-time, only a certain amount of ceremonial is dispensed with. At ordinary times the high-caste Hindu when he is away from home prepares his own dinner and eats it alone. Before cooking he bathes. Complete immersion is prescribed, preferably in natural running water. Where there is no stream or pool he is content with a wash down from a bucket; and as he washes he must repeat certain prayers, facing the east. While eating he wears nothing but his dhoti (loin cloth) and sacred thread; the upper part of his body and his feet are bare.

A small square is marked off for cooking. This is called the chauka. It is smoothed and plastered over, or lepai-ed as he calls it, with mud, or cowdung when available. Should anyone not of the caste touch the chauka after it has been prepared, all the food within its limits is defiled and must be thrown away.

There are two distinct kinds of food, kachi which is cooked in ghi, and pakhi which is cooked in water. Kachi may be eaten only at the chauka; but happily for the sepoy pakhi may be carried about and eaten anywhere; otherwise caste would completely demobilise him. Amongst Brahmans the caste convention of cooking their own food and eating it alone dies hard; and I know a Rajput class regiment in which it took ten years to introduce the messing system. Company cooking pots were accepted at first, but with no economy of space or time; for the vessels were handed round and each man used them to cook his own food in turn. The Brahmans are even more fastidious. I remember watching a class regiment at their meal in the Essin position; their habit of segregation had spread them over a wide area. Each man had ruled out his own pitch, and a Turk would have taken the battalion for a brigade. Only in the case of near relatives will two men sit at the same chauka. In spite of the cold, one or two of them were naked except for the loin cloth. The others wore vests of wool, which (apart from the loin cloth) is the one and only material that Brahmans may wear at meals. All had first bathed and changed their dhoti according to the prescribed rites, and carried water with them to wash off any impurity from their feet when they entered the chauka.

There are many prescribed minutiæ of ritual which vary with each sect and sub-tribe, but these are the main inhibitions. Even on service the Hindu preserves the sanctity of the chauka, and if not a Brahman, takes with him a Brahman cook, relaxes nothing in regard to the purity of his water from contamination by the wrong kind of people, and would rather starve than eat meat killed in an unorthodox way. The mutton or goat that the Mussalman eats must be slain by the halal or the stroke at the throat, and the mutton the Sikh or Hindu eats by the jatka or stroke at the back of the neck. The most elaborate precautions were taken in France and were observed in Mesopotamia and elsewhere, to keep the two kinds of meat separate. There was once a complaint that the flies from the Muhammadan butchery settled on the meat prepared for the Hindus, and the two slaughter-houses were accordingly removed farther apart. Orthodoxy in this point is no mere fad, but a genuine physical need born of centuries of tradition. The mere sight of the wrong kind of meat is nauseating to the fastidious, and in cases where it is not physically nauseating, toleration would be extremely bad form. I think the story has already been told of the Gurkha subadar on board the transport between Bombay and Marseilles who, when asked if his men would eat frozen meat, replied, after consulting them, "Sahib, they will have no objection whatever, provided one of them may be permitted each day to see the animal frozen alive."

On service, of course, as on pilgrimages under hard climatic conditions, there are dispensations in the ceremonial, though not in the essentials, of caste. Brahmans have fought for us from Plassey to the present day and their fastidious personal cleanliness has contributed to the smartness and discipline of the Indian Army. In early days, when the ranks of the

Bengal regiments were filled almost entirely with high-caste Hindus, orthodoxy was maintained in spite of all the rigours of war. To-day little has changed. Bathing when the nearest water is an icy glacier stream is not indulged in now on a frontier campaign; and where there is no water at all the sepoy does not lose caste by the neglect of his ablutions. The Rajput as a rule will eat his meals with his boots and clothes on, as he has done no doubt whenever he has been under arms since the Pandavas and Kouravas fought at Delhi.

The fastidious caste ceremonial is discouraged in the Indian Army. It leads to complications at all times, especially on a campaign; and a good Commanding Officer prides himself on his men's common sense and adaptability to environment. Yet there have been occasions, even among sepoys, when ritual and caste exclusiveness have been turned to disciplinary uses. Here is a story which is very much to the point. The first scene of this little drama was played in Egypt; the last on the banks of the Tigris.

There was a company of Rajputs somewhere in the neighbourhood of Suez, which contained a draft of very raw recruits. Three of these youngsters and a particularly callow lance-naik were holding a picquet on the east bank of the canal when they lost their heads. One of them blazed off at a shadow. He was frightened by the tamarisk bushes in the moonlight, and thought they were Turks' heads. A panic set in. All four blazed into the scrub, threw down their rifles, bolted as if the devil were behind them, and were only held up by the barbed wire of their own outpost. The jiwans were notoriously wild and jungly, and everything that a recruit should not be. They had never left their village save for a few months' training before they embarked on the transport in Bombay. A certain allowance might be made for stupidity and bewilderment, sufficient in the case of extreme youth to waive the death penalty. Had it been a moving campaign; had the regiment been in actual contact with the enemy, these young men would have been "for the wall." There is nothing else to do when soldiers go the wrong way. The O.C. and the Adjutant were considering how to deal with them when the Subadar-Major entered the orderly room. The man was a veteran, with a double row of ribbons on his breast, and he had never let the regiment down in all his service. He begged, as a special favour, that Rajput officers should be permitted to wipe out the stain. "Leave it to us, Sahib," he said: "we will put such an indignity on them, that there will not be a jiwan in the regiment who will shrink from bahadri * again." The Colonel saw the wisdom of this. The Rajput izzat was at stake, and he knew his man. So the Indian officers of the regiment were deputed to deal with the case themselves, just as prefects at school take the law into their own hands and administer it with a much more deterrent effect than the headmaster with his cane. The jiwans were tapped on the head with a slipper, the last ignominy that can befall a Rajput. After such disgrace they could not enter the chauka and mess with their caste companions. That is to say, they were socially excommunicated until their honour was retrieved. For nearly eighteen months they lit their outcast fire and took their meals apart at a measured distance from the chaukas—at such a distance that no ray of contamination could proceed from them to it.

They were still under the ban when the regi-

* Brave deeds.

ment left Egypt and went to Mesopotamia. They did not go into action until the relieving column found themselves in the impasse before Kut. This was their first chance, and all four rehabilitated themselves. Two died honourably, one of them inside the enemy's trenches killed by a Turkish grenadier; one was awarded the Indian Order of Merit; and the lance-naik degraded was promoted to naik. He was in the rearguard covering the retirement until dark, and it was noticed that he laid out all his cartridge cases as he fired, keeping them nicely dressed in a neat little heap, as had been well rubbed into him on parade. I am told that there is much promise in this jiwan. And it must be admitted that the caste instinct with all its disabilities made a man of him. Breeding brought into contact with regimental tradition gives the sense of *noblesse oblige*, and deference is the birthright of the twice-born. Thus the Brahman of Oudh, tried and proved in a wrestling match or a tug-of-war, thinks himself as good a man in a scrap as the most fire-eating Turk; and the assumption is all on the credit side.

Rajput pride is at the bottom of the saddest story of a sepoy I have ever heard. The man was not a Rajput of the plains, but a hill-man of Rajput descent, as brave a man as any in a battalion whose chivalry in France became a household word. After two days' incessant fighting with a minimum of rest at night, he fell asleep at his post. On account of his splendid service, and his exhaustion at the time, which was after all the tax of gallantry, the death penalty was commuted, and the man was sentenced to thirty lashes. He would much have preferred death. However, he took the lashes well, and there was little noticeable change in him afterwards beyond an increase of reserve. He went about his work as usual, and was in two or three more actions, in which he acquitted himself well. After a complete year in France, the battalion was moved to Egypt, where they stayed five months. Then came the welcome news that they were returning home. On the afternoon of the day he disembarked at Bombay the Rajput shot himself. He had chosen to live when there was work to do and death was his neighbour every day; now, when he might have lived, and when he was a bare three days from his family and home, he chose to die. The British officers tried to find out from the men what had driven him to it. But the sepoys were very silent and reticent. All they would say was that it was "on account of shame."

The boy who commanded his platoon, and who had been shooting with him in his district before the war, knows no more than I the processes of his mind. He is inclined to think that he decided at once, immediately after sentence had been executed, to destroy himself when his regiment returned. Or he may have turned it over in his mind day and night for more than a year, and in the end the sight of Hindustan resolved him. When the idea of home became real and imminent, the thought became unendurable that he should be pointed at in the village street as the man who had been whipped. In one case there is heroism; in the other a very human weakness; and in either case a tragedy of spirit that reveals the intensity of pride which is the birthright of the "twice-born."

THE GARHWALI

THE Garhwalis' *début* in Mesopotamia was worthy of their inspiring record in France. It was at Ramadie. They made the night march on September 27th, 1916, marched and fought all the 28th, and on the morning of the 29th carried the Aziziyah and Sheikh Faraja Ridges at the point of the bayonet, in an advance of 1500 yards under frontal and enfilade fire. The Sheik Faraja ridge was their objective. But this was not enough. The bridge of the Aziziyah Canal lay beyond, a point of vantage, for over it all guns or wheeled transport that escaped from Ramadie would have to pass. Feeling that they had rattled the Turk, that his tail was down, and that it was a moment when initiative might turn the scale, they pushed on another thousand yards over open ground, "as bald as a coot," crossed a deep nullah, seized the bridge, scuppered the teams of three Turkish guns, captured them, and accepted the surrender of a Turkish General and two thousand men.

To face p. 138.] THE GARHWALI.

Of course there was a lot of luck in it, but it was the luck that gallantry deserves and wins for itself and turns to account. The Turk was cornered and hemmed in with the cavalry astride the Aleppo road to the west, the Euphrates at his back and no bridge, and our infantry pressing in on the south and the east. But it was a wide front and our line was thin; by the time that they had reached the Canal the three assaulting companies were a bare hundred strong, and if the Turk had had the heart of the Garhwalis he would have rolled them up.

Standing by the captured guns, with the stalwart Turks coming in submissively all round, as if the surrender of the Anatolian to the Garhwali were a law of nature and a preordained thing, a subadar of the regiment turned modestly to his lieutenant and said, "Now it is all right, Sahib. I had my fears about the young men. They knew so little and were untried. Now we may be assured. They will stand."

When the battalion made the night march on September 27th, exactly two years and two days had passed since they had fought their last action in France; and they had seen more than one incarnation. The Subadar might well be anxious. The regiment had a large proportion of recruits, and they had a tall record to preserve. For the "gharry-wallah," or Indian cabby, as he is familiarly called, though he has never driven anything but the Hun—and the Turk, leapt into fame at Festubert, and has never lost an iota of his high repute. Before the war his name was unknown to the man in the street. The first battalion of the 39th Garhwal Rifles was raised in 1887—the second in 1901, and they had seen little service till France. Yet the Garhwali had always been a fighting man. He enlisted in the Gurkha regiments before the class battalions were formed, and his prowess helped to swell their fame, though one heard little or nothing of him. He was swallowed up and submerged in the Gurkha, and did not exist as a race apart. When at last the class regiments came into being he had to wait thirty years for his chance. But his officers knew him and loved him, and were confident all the while that his hour of recognition would come.

It came at Festubert, when the first battalion attacked and recaptured the lost trenches. Regiment after regiment had driven in the most determined counter-attacks across a thousand yards of snow-covered ground, and every assault had been withered up by the enemy's fire. The Garhwalis got in on the flank, working along trenches held by our own troops to the left of those captured by the Germans. They carried traverse after traverse, and the taking of every traverse was as the taking of a fort. At first they had a bagful of "jampot" bombs hastily contrived by the Sappers—it was long before the days of Mills and Stokes and other implements of destruction; but the bombs soon gave out, and for the long stretch of trench, 300 yards or more, it was nothing but rifle and bayonet work. A few men would leap on the parapet and parados at each traverse, and then the party in the trench would charge round the traverse and dispatch the garrison with the bayonet until the whole line was in our hands. These are familiar tactics to-day, but trench warfare was then in its infancy, and it fell to the Garhwalis to give the lead and point the way. The gallant Naik Dewan Singh Negi, who led his men round traverse after traverse and evicted the Hun, was awarded the V.C.

That was in the last week of November,

1914. For the next few months the Garhwalis were tried and proved every day. Neither the severe conditions of the winter, nor the strange and terrible phenomena of destruction evolved in the new Armageddon, could damp his fighting spirit. But it was on the 10th March, 1915, when the two battalions "went over the top" at Neuve Chapelle, that the name of Garhwal, no longer obscure, became a name to conjure with in France. Ever since that day the Garhwali has stood in the very front rank in reputation among the fighting classes of the Indian Army. The 1st Battalion charged a line of trenches where the wire was still uncut. Every British officer and nearly every Indian officer in the attacking line was killed, but the men broke through the wire, bayoneted the garrison of the trench, and hung on all that day from 8 a.m. to 6 p.m. with no Sahib in command. The C.O. and Adjutant were both wounded, and at nightfall two officers were sent across from the 2nd Battalion, who had got through with less severe loss, to help the shattered remnants of the 1st. They hung on all that night and the next day, and beat off a heavy counter-attack on the morning of the 12th. Rifleman Gobar Singh was awarded the V.C. for his day's work on the 10th, when he led the front line bayoneting the Hun, but the gallant sepoy never lived to wear his award.

The Garhwali subadar who went over the field with us after the Ramadie fight, said to his officer that the regiment had not had such a day since the "charge-ki-din." The 10th of March at Neuve Chapelle is remembered by the Garhwali as "the day of the charge." For them it is THE day. Even Ramadie will not wipe it out with all its fruits of victory. For the regiment was put to a grimmer test at Neuve Chapelle, and the reward in the measure of honour could not possibly be surpassed. Still it was good to see that the new lot was as staunch as the first. They are a modest-looking crowd, some of the youngest mere boys without a wrinkle on their faces. The veterans reminded me very much of Gurkhas, but more of the Khas Ghurka, who is half a Rajput, than of the Magar or Gurung. The Garhwalis, like the Dogras, are direct descendants of the Rajputs who cut out kingdoms for themselves in the hills centuries ago. There is no Mongol blood in them, save in the case of intermarriage with Nepal. They are a distinct race, yet being hillmen and neighbours, they naturally have much in common with the Gurkha, in habit as well as look. They have the cheerfulness and simplicity of the Gurkha, and the same love of a scrap for its own sake, and, what is more endearing, the same inability to grow up. They are always children. They care nothing for drill books and maps, and as often as not hold them upside down. But they see red in a fight, and go for anything in front of them. Both battalions would have been wiped out a dozen times had it not been for their British officers.

There is in build a great deal in common between the Gurkha and Garhwali, and confusion is natural in the uninitiated. It is not only that both are hillmen, belong to rifle regiments, and wear slouch or terai hats; the Garhwali is in appearance a cross between the Dogra and the "Ghurk." He has the close-cropped hair, the "bodi" or topknot, the hillman's face, and you will find in the veterans the same tight-drawn lines under the eye that bespeak stiffening in a hard school and give them a grim and warlike look. But the British officer in a Garhwali regiment naturally resents the swallowing of the small community, with its honour, prestige, individuality and all, by the great. The Garhwali, he argues, has at least earned his right to a separate identity now, and he is jealous of the overshadowing wing.

Ramadie was a great day for him. The Garhwalis did not win the battle, but they reaped the rich field by the bridge alone. Other regiments did splendid work that day, and the officer who showed me over the ground was afraid that I should forget them in "booming his show." "It was just our luck," he explained, "that we happened to be there." Most of the 90th Punjabis had side-tracked to the right to take Unjana Hill, while the rest of the brigade swept on and cleared the Sheikh Faraja Ridge. To gain the Aziziyah Canal the Garhwalis changed direction and bore off to the left. Other companies came up afterwards, but when the Garhwalis reached the bridge they were unsupported. They took the bridge, the guns, the 2000 prisoners, the Turkish General,* alone. As for the prisoners, "It was not so much a capture," the officer explained to me modestly, "as a surrender to the nearest troops, and we happened to be there."

* The Commander, Ahmed Bey, surrendered to the 90th Punjabis.

I had watched them in the distance, black specks on the sand, but it was not until I went over the field with them the next day, and they fought the battle again, that I realised what they had done. As the Garhwalis charged over the open from Sheikh Faraja Ridge, the three guns in front of them, firing point-blank over their sights, poured in shrapnel, raking the ground, churning up the sand in a deadly spray. Half-way across there was a deep dry nullah, with steep banks and a few scattered palms on the other side. It was an ideal place to hold, but the enemy were slipping away. In a moment the Garhwalis were in the nullah, clambered up the opposite bank, and had their Lewis-gun trained on the gun teams at 400 yards. The Turkish gunners died game, and in the Garhwalis' last burst over the flat not a man fell. They rushed the palm-clump to the right of the guns and the guns, which were undefended with their dead all round. The three pieces were intact. The Turks had no time to damage them. The horses were all saddled up in the palms, with the ammunition limbers, officers' charges, mules and camels. Very quickly the Garhwalis dug a pot-hook trench round the guns and palm-clump, watched eagerly for the supports, and waited for the counter-attack which surely must come. The three assaulting companies were a bare hundred strong now, and behind the mud walls five hundred yards in front of them, though they did not know it, lay the Turkish General and 2000 of his men. But the silencing of the guns was the beginning of the collapse. The Turks knew the game was up. The iron ring we were drawing round them, their unsuccessful sortie against the cavalry in the night, had taken the heart out of them. No doubt they thought the Garhwalis the advance-guard of a mighty host.

White flags appeared on the mud wall in front. A small group of Turks came out unarmed. Eight men were sent to bring them in. Then a "crocodile" emerged from the nullah. "I've seen some crocodiles," a very junior subaltern said to me, "but I have never seen one which bucked me like that." The monster grew and swelled until it assumed enormous proportions. One could not see whence each new fold of the beast proceeded. It was like dragon seed conjured up out of invisibility in the desert by a djinn. But it was a very tame dragon and glad of its captivity. And there was really something of a miracle in it,—the kind of miracle that happens in a legend or at the end of a fairy tale, where the moral is pointed of the extraordinary rewards that befall all the young who are single-minded and unafraid. Half an hour after the crocodile had collected its folds Ahmed Bey, the Turkish General, was discovered in a neighbouring house, and surrendered to a young British officer of the company.

When they saw the Turkish General coming in, all the jiwans (young men) must have thought of the "charge-ki-din," the day of honour of which they had inherited the tradition but not the memory, and wished they had been there too.

THE KHATTAK

THE Khattaks kept their spirits up all through the hot weather. They were too lively sometimes. There was one man who imitated a three-stringed guitar a few yards from my tent as an accompaniment to his friend's high treble. One night after a good feed, when the shamal began blowing, they broke out into one of their wild dances, after the Dervish fashion, swinging swords and leaping round the bonfire. You would think the Khattak would be up to any murder after this kind of show, but I am told the frenzy works the offending Adam out of him.

I was watching a fatigue party working at a bund on a particularly sultry afternoon. They were all a bit "tucked up," but as soon as the dhol (drum) and serinai (oboe) sounded, they started cat-calling and made the earth fly. The Khattak is as responsive to the serinai as the Highlander to the regimental slogan, but he is more demonstrative. It is a good thing to be by, when the —— Rifles leave camp. At the first sound of the dhol and serinai the Khattak company breaks into a wild treble shriek, tailing off perhaps with the bal-bala, the Pathan imitation of the gurgling of the camel. The Sikh comes in with his "Wah Guru-ji-Ki-Khalsa, Wah Guru-ji-Ki-jai!" and the Punjabi mussalman with his "Allah, Allah, Allah, Allah"; or he may borrow the Khattak's bal-bala, or the British "Hip, hip, hooray!"

The Khattak is impulsive, mercurial, easily excited, seldom dispirited, and if so, only for a short time. His élan is sometimes a positive danger during an attack. At Sheikh Saad, on the right bank on January 7th, it was difficult to hold the Khattak company back while the regiment on their left was coming up; they were all for going on ahead and breaking the line; and in the end it was a premature sortie of the Khattaks that precipitated the assault.

Shere Ali was among these. He and his father, Shahbaz Khan of the Bhangi Khel, were typical Khattaks. From these two one may gather a fair estimate of the breed. Shahbaz Khan, the father, I did not meet. Shere Ali

I saw wounded on a barge at Sheikh Saad. He was introduced to me by his machine-gun officer, who was wounded at the same time.

Father and son both served in the Khattak double company of the —— Rifles. Shahbaz Khan, retired subadar, died after eighteen months of the Great War without hearing a shot fired. It was very galling to the old man to be out of it, for his idea of bliss was a kind of glorified Armageddon. He had fought in Tochi and Waziristan, but these frontier scraps were unsatisfying. "It was only playing at war," he said. He longed for a padshah-ki-lerai, "a war of kingdoms," in the old Mahabharat style. "Sahib," he said, "I should like to be up to my knees in gore with thousands of dead all round me." But the old man was born fifteen years too soon. He would have been happy in the night attack upon Beit Aieesa, or even perhaps with Shere Ali on the right bank at Sheikh Saad, when the regiment rushed the Turkish trenches.

Shere Ali was with the regiment in Egypt, left the canal with them in December, 1915, and was just in time for the advance from Ali Gharbi. Shahbaz Khan came down to the depôt and dismissed his son with envious blessings. He had dyed his beard a bright red, and he carried himself with a youthful air, hoping that the Colonel might discover some subterfuge by which he could re-emerge on the active list. The Colonel would have given ten of his jiwans for him, and Shahbaz Khan knew it. But the rules were all against him. So the regiment went off to the accompaniment of the dhol and serinai, amidst many loud shouts and salutations, mingled with British cheers, and old Shahbaz Khan was left behind. He died in his bed before Shere Ali came back, and no doubt a brooding sense of having been born too soon hastened his end.

Father and son, I have explained, were faithful to type. The Khattak is the Celt of the Indian Army, feckless, generous, improvident, mercurial, altogether a friendly and responsive person, but with the queer kink in him you get in all Pathans, that primitive sensitive point of honour or shame which puzzles the psychologist. It is often his duty to kill a man. On these occasions the ægis of the British Government is a positive misfortune. For the Khattaks are mainly a cis-frontier race, and therefore subject to all the injustice and inequalities of our law. Citizenship of the Empire hampers the blood feud. A stalking duel started in British territory generally ends in the Andamans or Paradise. If you lose you lose, and if you win you may be hanged or deported for life. Nevertheless, the instinct for honour survives this discouragement, and there is a genial colony of Khattak outlaws over the border.

Old Shere Khan killed a rival for his wife's affections in the regimental lines, and he could not have done anything else. The man's offence carried its own sentence in the minds of all decent-thinking people. The Subadar-Major begged the Adjutant to cut the fellow's name—Sher Gol, I think it was—and to get him well away before night. Otherwise, he said, there would be trouble. But the Adjutant could not look into the case before the next morning. In the meantime, to safeguard Sher Gol, he told the Subadar to see that twenty stout men slept round his bed. The Subadar made it fifty, but the quarter guard would have been better; for at one in the morning—it was a late guest-night—the Adjutant and Sher Gol's company commander were called out quietly to see the remains of him. His head was swaying slowly from side to side on the edge of the bed. A hatchet planted in the skull and oscillating with every movement of it had been left there as evidence. The Subadar put his knee against the charpoy (bed) and pulled the chopper out. Whereupon Sher Gol opened his eyes, saying, "Ab roshni hai" ("Now there is light"), and expired. He had been killed with fifty men sleeping round him. They had all slept like the dead and nobody had heard the blow. There was no evidence against Shahbaz Khan whatever; public opinion was on his side.

Of such stock was Shere Ali, and though a mere lad he had killed his man at Kohat before he fought at Sheikh Saad. Zam, zan, zar (land, women, and gold), according to the Persian proverb, are at the bottom of all outrages, and with Shahbaz Khan and Shere Ali, as with nine Khattaks out of ten, it was zan. And zan (woman), too, was in Shere Ali's mind when he brooded so dejectedly over his wound at Sheikh Saad. He was hit in the foot and lamed the moment he left the trenches. This meant a two-inch shortage, and, as he believed, permanent crutches.

"I have never seen him so down in the mouth," Anderson, the machine-gun officer, said to me on the barge. "He has lost all his cheery looks."

Shere Ali was certainly dispirited. He had his head and chest low, and all the wind taken out of him. He looked like a bird with its crest down and its feathers ruffled.

The Khattak thinks no end of his personal appearance. He dresses to kill, and loves to go and swank in the bazaar in his gala kit. He will spend hours over his toilet peering at himself in the glass, all the while without a trace of self-consciousness, though his neighbours may be almost as interested in the performance as he. Then when his hair is neatly oiled and trim to the level of the lobe of his ear, he will stride forth in his flowery waistcoat of plum-colour or maroon velvet with golden braid, spotless white baggy trousers, a flower behind his ear, a red handkerchief in his pocket, a cane in his hand, and for headgear a high Kohat lungi—black with yellow and crimson ends, and a kula* covered with gold.

Every Khattak is a bit of a blood, and Shere

* The peak which protrudes from the centre of the turban.

Ali was true to type. In his country a showy exterior betokens the gallant in both senses of the word. A woman of parts will not look at a man unless he has served in the army, or is at least something of a buccaneer. Of course, a wound honourably come by is a distinction, and Shere Ali should not have been depressed. He would return a bahadur, I told him, but he only smiled sadly. He was crippled; there was no getting over it. He would join in the Khattak dance no more. As for the dhol and serinai—if that intriguing music had broken out just then I believe we should both have wept.

I heard more of Shere Ali from Anderson when he returned fit three months afterwards. In the depôt the lad's depression seemed permanent. He was very anxious to get back to his village, and kept on asking when he might go. But he was told that he must wait for a special pair of boots. He was sent to Lahore to Watts to be fitted.

"Give him the best you can turn out," the Adjutant wrote; "a pair that will last at least three years." Shere Ali returned all impatience.

"I have been measured, Sahib," he said;

"but I have not yet got the boots. Now may I go back to my village."

"No," the Adjutant told him, "you must wait for the boots. We must see you well fitted out first."

He had another weary two weeks to wait. He was evidently rather bored with all this fuss about footgear. What good are boots to a man who can't walk?

At last they came. He untied the box with melancholy indifference, threw the tissue paper and cardboard on the floor, and examined them resignedly.

"Sahib," he said, "there is some mistake—they are not a pair."

He was persuaded to put them on.

"Now walk," the Adjutant said.

Shere Ali rose with an effort, and was leaning forward to pick up his crutches, when he noticed that his lame foot touched ground. He advanced it gingerly, stamped with it once or twice in a puzzled way, and then began doubling round the orderly room. The Adjutant said that his chest visibly filled out and the light came back to his eyes. He took a step forward and saluted.

"When is the next parade, Sahib?" he asked.

"Never mind about parades," the Adjutant told him. "Go back to your village and bring us some more jiwans like yourself, as many as you like, and keep on bringing them."

We can't have too many Khattaks. Shere Ali, I am told, has quite a decent stride. He is no end of a bahadur. And he is a sight for the gods in his white baggy trousers, flowery waistcoat, and Kohat lungi, when he dresses to kill.

THE HAZARA

I THOUGHT I had met all the classes in the Indian Army. But one day at Sheikh Saad, when I was half asleep with the heat, I opened my eyes to see a company of unfamiliar faces. They were not unfamiliar individually. I had met the double of each of them; yet collectively they were unfamiliar. In the first platoon I could have sworn to a Gurkha, a Chinaman, a Tibetan, a Lepcha of Sikkim, a Chilasi, and an undoubted Pathan with a touch of the Turki in him.

Whether in eye, nose, complexion, or the flatness of the cheek there was something Mongol in them all, while in at least half there was a suggestion of the Semitic. The Lepcha had the innocent jungly glance of the cowherd of Gantok or Pemiongchi; the Chinaman with the three-cornered eyes was an exaggeration of type; the Pathan would have passed muster in the Khyber Rifles. They were all fairer than many

Englishmen after a year of Mesopotamia, and they spoke a kind of mongrel Persian with a Tibetan intonation.

The regiment disembarked from the steamer and filed out to the rest camp behind my tent in the intense heat of a September afternoon. It was too hot to sleep, much too hot to wander about and ask questions. If it had been cooler I should have gone out and talked to one of the regimental officers. But 118 degrees in the shade under canvas kills curiosity. I remember there was a dog under the outside fly of my tent, and for half an hour I mistook its breathing for the engine of a motor-car, but never quite rose to the effort of getting up to see if the machine could not be persuaded to move on. Happily there was no need to go out and ask who these men were. I soon tumbled to it, though I had never seen the breed until they landed in the blinding glare of Sheikh Saad.

The history of the Hazaras is written in their faces. They are of Mongol origin, though the colony is settled near Ghazni in Afghanistan. I had heard how they came there, but had forgotten the story, only remembering that the Mongols had married wives of the country of

To face p. 160.]

THE HAZARA.

their adoption. Hence the curious blend of the Central Asian and the Jew in the crowd that was stumbling up the bank. A little reflection solved the puzzle in spite of the heat.

There was one small tamarisk bush, not more than eighteen inches high, but where it stood on the edge of the bank it threw a four-foot patch of shade; the only natural shadow to be had anywhere round. A sepoy of the regiment appropriated this. Then a jemadar came up and demanded it for himself. The sepoy pretended not to hear. "Go and relieve the sentry," his officer said, pointing to an erect figure in the sun who was being broiled by inches, "over the kit pile there by the steamer. Look alive. Clear out!" The Hazara dragged himself out of the shade, and approaching his friend the guard, caught him a resounding whack on the ear. One cannot strike an officer; yet something had to be done; one has to let steam off somehow. The guard jabbed at him with the bayonet and took himself off in good spirit. The jemadar laughed.

All this horseplay was characteristic of everything I had heard of the Hazara. The psychology of it was not of the East. There was something Cockney or Celtic in the blows taken in good part, the give and take, the common-sense and easy-going humour of the scene.

In the evening I went over and had a chat with the Hazara. One or two of them spoke Hindustani with the accent of a Tommy, calling me "Sabb." Finding them friendly and communicative folk, I asked them their history. They had come over with a Ghenghiz Khan, they told me, to sack Delhi; all agreed that it was Ghenghiz Khan, and that it was about 800 years ago and that they had crossed the Karakoram, and that their own particular ancestors had been left by the Khan to hold the outpost of Ghazni in Afghanistan. I looked up their history afterwards and found that they had given it me more or less as it is set down in the text-books.

Also I learnt that it is not easy for the Hazaras to leave Afghanistan. The Amir's guards have orders to hold them up at the frontier, though there are time-honoured ways in which they contrive to break the cordon, bribing the guards or slipping through in disguise, generally with the Powindah caravans. It is still more difficult for them to get home and return when on leave, and this is an embargo which indulges the Hazara's natural bent for travel. In the furlough season you will find him as far afield from cantonments as he can get in the time, often as far as Colombo, Calcutta, Madras, or Rangoon. Filthy lucre is not his motive. What he earns he spends. He has a curiosity uncommon in the Asiatic. He likes wandering and seeing the world for its own sake; he lives comfortably, is a bit of a spendthrift, gambles a lot, dresses with an air, and likes to cut a figure in a tonga where the ordinary sepoy would save a few annas by going on foot. If he belongs to a Pioneer regiment he can afford it. For the Pioneer works on a Government contract in peace time, and the Hazara thinks he has fallen on a poor job if he cannot make twelve annas extra for a day's work in addition to his pay.

Few of them can read or write, but though illiterate they are keen-witted and speak with the terseness of a proverb. They are much quicker "at the uptake" than the Gurkha, whom they resemble in many ways. When they go to Kirkee for Pioneer training they generally come out top in the machine-gun, musketry, and signalling courses, and they make excellent surveyors. As Pioneers they are hard to beat.

It will be gathered from the incident of the sepoy who was dispossessed of his tamarisk bush, that the Hazara is of a cheerful disposition. There is generally a comedian in the regiment, and after dinner at Sheikh Saad one of the men was called in to give us a kind of solo-pantomime. He began with the smart salute of the sepoy, bringing his hand down with the mechanical click of a bolt; then he gave us the Sahib's casual lifting of the cane, next he was a havildar drilling a raw recruit. He took the parts in turn and contrived some clever fooling. But I gathered that the man was only second-rate. No sooner had he made his exit than everybody in the mess lamented Faizo who beguiled so many nights of the New Zealanders on the canal, a subtle artist compared to this clown with his stock regimental turns. Faizo is the castigator of pretence, scourge of hypocrisy and the humbug of the Church. In one scene he is the shaven mullah abstractedly mumbling his prayers while he intently prepares his food. A dog comes in and defiles the dish, Faizo for the moment becomes the dog—then the mullah torn with the fury of commination, pursuing the dog with oaths and missiles and spurning the polluted food. Then the mullah again, hungry and unctuously sophisticated, blessing the food, miraculously restoring its virtue, and finding it good.

No one is better at a nickname than Faizo. Few men are known in the regiment by the name their father gave them. They are remembered by some oddity or unhappy lapse of conduct, or the place they come from, and Faizo is the regimental godfather of them all. There is Mahomet Ulta—Mahomet upside down—who always gets hold of the wrong end of the stick; Ser Khuskh—the dry-head, and "The Mullah," and "Kokri Gulpusht," "the frog with a shining posterior," who looks as if his face had been glazed. Also there is Ghulam Shah the "Maygaphon." This is how he came by the name.

Ghulam Shah is that rare thing, a stupid Hazara—and what is worse a stupid havildar. One day on manœuvres he had tied the Hazaras up in an inextricable knot through misunderstanding some command. The Colonel stood on a mound and cursed him from afar off, and as his language became more violent Ghulam Shah became more confused. He stood on one leg and then on the other. Then remembering the megaphone he carried he put it to his ear, and lastly, in despair, to his eye. On the evening of the field day Faizo borrowed the regimental megaphone and pursued the wretched Ghulam Shah round the parade ground. Ghulam Shah was a fat man who ran heavily and panted. Faizo put the instrument to his ear and to his eye. He inspected him with a theatrical gesture of his disengaged hand. He listened to him curiously, as though he was some strange beast. Last insult of all, he put the megaphone to his nose and smelt him.

It was refreshing to see how the Hazaras kept their spirits up in this firepit, and to hear the clipped Mongol speech of the tableland in the plain of Iraq. At Sheikh Saad we were little more than a hundred miles from the plain of Shinar and the site of the Tower of Babel, and we were carrying on with a confusion of tongues that would have demobilised the tower builders. Here was a man talking Persian like a Tibetan, and from beyond the circle of light there penetrated to us the most profane comments delivered in the homeliest Devonshire burr.

Among the Hazaras were Baltis, who are being recruited into the Hazara battalion now. Their country, Baltistan, or Little Tibet, lies to the north of Kashmir, between Fadakh and the Gilgit district. The Baltis, too, have a distinct language of their own and come of a semi-Mongolian stock, and are Shiahs by faith like the Hazaras. They were originally polygamists, like their neighbours the Bhots of Fadakh, but when they became Muhammadans they adopted polyandry. They resemble the Hazaras in looks, but on the whole are shorter and darker. They are an extremely hardy race, and eke out a very scanty living as coolies and tillers of the soil in the valleys of the Indus and its tributaries up Skardu and Shigar way—a happy hunting-ground, the mere thought of which gave one an empty and homesick feeling inside when tied down to one's gridiron or Iraq. I had seen them at work in the high snow passes of Tibet, their natural home, and little expected to meet them in the malignant waste by the Tigris, which one would have thought must be death to mountain-born folk whose villages are seldom found at an altitude of less than 8000 feet above the sea. Yet the descent to Tartarus did not seem to have dismayed them in the least.

The Hazara is probably the nearest approach to the European you will find in the Indian Army. It is odd that a cross of the Mongol and Semitic should have produced this breed. His leg is not of the East; he walks like the Tyke. I do not know the Tartar in his home, but these descendants of his have much in common with us. In his sense of humour, quick temper, rough and tumble wrestling, ragging and practical jokes, and practical common sense; in his curiosity and love of travel, in his complexion and disposition and in his easy-going habits of life, the Hazara is not so very far removed from an Islander of the West.

The Hazara has a good opinion of himself though his pride is unobtrusive. He is hard as nails, a man of tremendous heart, and he is not easily beaten in a trial of physical strength. They nearly always pull off the divisional tug-of-war. In the two mixed-company battalions that enlist Hazaras it is a recognised tradition that the light-weights should be a purely Hazara team.

There is not much material as yet for an

estimate of the military virtue of the race, but according to all precedent they should prove good men in a scrap. For the Hazara is an anomaly in the East, where men as a rule are only stout-hearted and self-respecting where they are lords of the soil and looked up to by their neighbours. In Afghanistan, as alien subjects of the Amir, Shiahs among Sunnis, Mongols among Pathans, they have held their heads high and proved themselves unbroken in spirit; though living isolated and surrounded by hostile peoples, and from time to time the objects of persecution, you will find few types of manhood less browbeaten than the Hazara.

THE MER AND MERAT

THE Hindu and Muhammadan Mers and Merats from the Merwara Hills round Ajmere are men of curious customs and antecedents, very homely folk, and as good friends to the British Government as any children of the Empire. I met them first at Qurnah, in June, 1916; thin, lithe men with sparse beards like birds' nests in a winter tree. You could not tell the Mer from the Merat. They are of one race, and claim to be the issue of a Rajput king—Prithi Raj, I believe—by a Meena woman,—a mythical ancestry suggested no doubt by Brahmans in order to raise their social standing among other Hindus. They are really the descendants of the aboriginal tribes of Rajputana, but in course of time, through intercourse with Rajput Thakurs as servants, cultivators, and irregular levies, they have imbibed a certain amount of Rajput blood. They are a democratic crowd, and have never owed allegiance to the princes of Rajasthan.

To face p. 170.] THE MERAT.

Nor have they been defeated by them. In the old days when they made a foray the Rajput cavaliers would drive them back into their impossible country, where among their rocks and trees they would hurl defiance in the shape of stones and arrows at mounted chivalry. Then in the middle of last century an Englishman came along and did everything for them which a true friend can do. Like Nicholson, he became incorporated in the local Pantheon. He gave the Mers a statute and a name, and lamps are still burning at his shrine.

Mota is a Mer. There are six regiments in the Indian Army that draw from his community, one class and five company class battalions. But as Mota is an exaggeration of type, and more blessed with valour than brains and discretion, I will not say to what particular battalion he belonged.

When I saw Mota Jemadar he was rehearsing a part. His Colonel and I were sitting on the roof of a mud Arab house, then a regimental mess, where we had established ourselves for the evening, hoping to find some movement in the stifling air. Looking down we saw the jemadar doubling painfully and deliberately across the walled palm grove in a temperature of 105 degrees in the shade. We thought at first the man had been bitten by a scorpion or a snake, and the Colonel called out to him from the roof, "What is the matter, Mota?" "Nothing is the matter, Sahib," he called up, "I am practising for the Victaria Crarse."

The Colonel smiled and sighed. He knew his man, and he told me what these preparations impended. The regiment was new to the country and to war, and I gathered that unless otherwise instructed the jemadar would go over the parapet the first time he found himself in action, doubling along clumsily in the same determined fashion as if he had been propelled mechanically from behind, and that he would not pull up or look round until he got to the enemy's trenches. And he would do this with the full expectation of having the glittering cross pinned on his breast in the evening. The other alternative would not trouble his head.

Also I gathered that the phrase "unless otherwise instructed" implied much uphill work on the part of the regimental officer. Mota was imbued with a fixed idea. His mind was not in that receptive mood which enables the fighting man to act quickly in an emergency. Supposing his rôle were not the offensive. Supposing that he were suddenly attacked at the moment when he felt himself secure, and had no time for deliberation or counsel, the old jemadar might be doubling in any direction under the contagion of example or to reach a place where he could think out the new situation and resolve how to act. When a Mer gets as far as a rehearsal he will never fail in the performance. He is all right so long as he knows exactly what he is expected to do.

There was the historic occasion of Ajmere in 1857, when the action of the Mers and Merats altered the whole course of the Mutiny in their own district, and held back the wave that threatened to sweep over Rajasthan. News came to the local battalion that the garrison had risen at Nasirabad and murdered the British officers. Led by their Sahib and lawgiver, the Mers made a forced march of thirty-eight miles from Beawar to Ajmere, dispossessed the mutinous guards of the treasury and arsenal, and held the fort against the rebels who were advancing upon the city, flushed with success, from Nasirbad. All of which fell in with the

Mer legend that they would never be ruled by any save a white king.

It was a class battalion that I met at Qurnah in June, 1916; incidentally it was not Mota's crowd. They had already seen much hard campaigning, and a small scrap or two in the desert between the Kharkeh and Karum rivers, where some of the regiment had died of thirst. But the most interesting point about the Mers and Merats to a student of Indian races is the relationship between the Hindus and Muhammadans of the same stock. In the chapter about the Brahmans and Rajputs in the Army I have given an instance of how the caste system strengthened discipline. Caste, of course, is in itself a discipline, and was originally imposed as such. In its call for the sacrifice of the individual to the community it has played its part in the stiffening of the Hindu for countless generations. But in the twentieth century the most orthodox will admit its disabilities, the exacting ritual involved in it, and the artificial and complex differentiation between men who have really everything in common. The caste question as a rule, when it emerges in a regiment, creates difficulties, and very rarely, as in the case of the excommunicated Rajputs, smooths them over. The Merwara battalion, which was once divided by caste into two camps, is a case in point. It is an old story, but as it is little known it is worth recording as an example of the evils of exclusiveness. And as both parties are now good friends, no harm can be done by telling it.

First it should be understood that the Mers and Merats are the most home-staying folk in the Indian Army. Like the Gurkhas, the class battalion has one permanent cantonment, and never leaves it except to go on active service. Until this war they had not been on a campaign since the Afghan expedition in 1878–9. They are even more domiciled than the Gurkha, for their depôt at Ajmere is in their own district, and they can get home on a week-end's leave from Friday night till Monday morning; and when their turn comes they seldom let the privilege go by.

Living and serving in their own country, detached from other folk, they evolved a happy easy-going, tolerant, social system of their own. The Mers are Hindus; the Merats Muhammadans. They are of the same stock, but the Mussalman Merats are the descendants of the

Mers who were forcibly converted to Islam by Aurungzeb. This conversion did not break up the brotherhood. Hindu and Muhammadan intermarried, and sat at meals together within the chauka as before. It is no doubt on account of their freedom from the restrictions of both religions that the Merats have never reverted to Mers or become Muhammadans in real earnest. They still feared the Hindu deities, and were strangers to the inside of a mosque. Mer and Merat together made up a very united people, and one quite apart. They cared little for dogma or ritual, and had their own ideas about caste. Thus they lived contentedly together until 1904, when a party of them were sent home to England with other details of the Indian Army to attend the Coronation of King Edward VII.

It is sad to think that this happy anniversary should have been the beginning of discord, but the serpent entered their Eden when they took train to Bombay and embarked on the transport. Here they found themselves amongst every kind of sepoy from the Mahratta of the Konkan to the Jharwa of Assam, from the Bhangi Khel of Kohat to the Mussalman of Southern Madras—

all of whom had their prescribed ritual and fixed rules of life. Few of this crowd had ever seen the sea before, but they were most of them travelled men of the world compared to the Mer and Merat. Amongst the Rajputs, Gurkhas, Sikhs, Pathans, and Punjabi Mussalmans, the Ajmere contingent must have appeared the most open-mouthed and bewildered of country cousins. None of the sepoys knew anything about them. "Who are you? Where do you come from?" they were asked. They were just like children torn from the bosom of the family and plunged for the first time into the unsympathetic entourage of a school. They were twitted unmercifully for their unnatural alliance. Asked to define themselves they stated, quite honestly, that they were Rajputs. The easy-going Hindus made a huge joke out of this; the orthodox were angry and rude. For whoever saw a Rajput and a Mussalman break bread together? The Mer was told that he was not a true Rajput, not even a true Hindu. The poor Merats, too, were regarded as blacksliders from Islam. They did all sorts of things that a good Muhammadan ought not to do. All their old customs and easy compromises, all the happy little family understandings, those recognised and cherished inconsistences which make half the endearments of home-life, became the subject of an unfeeling criticism.

Mer and Merat became mutually suspicious. Before they reached Aden the Mers had already begun to dress their hair differently, more in the Rajput style. At Suez they were in two distinct camps. The cooking-vessels which had been common to both were abhorred by the Hindus; neither would eat what the other had touched; each eyed the other askance.

When they returned to India the infection of exclusiveness spread, and Hindu sectarian missionaries coming into the fold added to the mischief. But happily common sense and old affections prevailed. Now they do not ostensibly feed together and intermarry; but they are good friends, and relations are smooth, though they can never be quite the same happy family again.

Two generations or more of regimental life have passed since these events, and I heard a very different story of a Merwara company on board a transport in this war. When they embarked in Karachi harbour they trod the deck of the vessel tentatively and with suspicion. But soon timidity gave place to pride. "You see, Sahib," the Subadar explained, "we are not laid out by this sea-sickness which we are told is very disastrous to certain classes of sepoys, and even to some sahibs." The unknown peril had been the theme of conversation most of the way from Rajputana, and the Mers, no doubt, believed that the first entries in the "Regimental Roll of Honour" would be the victims of the subtle and malignant paralysis with which Kala pani (the black water) can infect the strongest. As bad luck would have it, no sooner had the transport cleared the harbour than they struck dirty weather and a choppy sea. Mer and Merat collapsed as one. On the third day those who had legs to support them or strength to stir the pot were carrying round food to the less fortunate, united in this common emergency and careless of caste and creed. The sea separated them, and ten years afterwards the sea joined them again. Let us hope that the voyage marked a revival of the golden age.

The story of both voyages bears out the comment of Mota's Colonel, that the Mer and Merat, though far from being impressionable, are singularly open to example. These brave and friendly folk may be lacking in initiative, but give them a lead, show them what may be done, and they will never fail in emulation. Hardly a man of military age is not enlisted, and the traditious of Ajmere were continued at Kut, where there was a company of Mers and Merats in one of the two regiments who held the liquorice factory so gallantly through the siege.

THE RANGHAR

The Mussalmans of Rajput descent are a fine fighting stock. The best known are the Ranghars of the Eastern Punjab and the Kaim Khanis of Rajputana proper. The handsomest sepoy I met in Mesopotamia was a Ranghar, and he had that jolly, dare-devil look about him which recalls the best traditions of the highwayman.

When the non-military Hindus, most of them unwilling converts, embraced Muhammadanism, it was the custom in choosing their Islamic name to adopt the prefix "Sheikh." Alma Ram became Sheikh Ali, for instance, and Gobind Das Sheikh Zahur-ud-din. But the proud Rajput warriors were unwilling to be classed with these. "We come of a fighting stock," they argued, "like the Pathans. Our history is more glorious than theirs." So they adopted the suffix "Khan," which with the man of genuine Muhammadan ancestry implies Pathan descent. The Chohans, when they became converted, were known to the Rajputs as the Kaim Khanis, or "the firm and unbreakable ones." Every Ranghar, too, was be-khaned, and as a class they have shown a martial spirit equal to the title.

The British officer in the Indian Cavalry swears by the Ranghars. I know cavalry leaders who would unhesitatingly name him if asked in what breed they considered there was the best makings of a sowar. He is born horseman and horsemaster. And he is very much "a man." Even in the Punjab, where there are collected the best fighting stocks in India—that is to say, the best fighting stocks in the East—he is a hero of romance. "You'll find the Ranghar," the Pirrhai tells us,

> "In the drink shop, or in the jail,
> On the back of a horse,
> Or in the deep grave."

I had heard that tag long before I met the Ranghar on service, and I wanted to see how his dare-devil, undisciplined past—if indeed it was as dare-devil as it is painted—served him on a campaign. The Ranghar, one knows, is a Rajput by origin and a Muhammadan by faith. His ancestors were brought to see eye to eye

To face p. 182.] THE RANGHAR.

with the Mogul—a change of vision due to no priestcraft, but dictated by the sword. It must be remembered that their lands were exposed to the full tide of the Moslem flood. The Rajputs who earned immortality by their defiance of Akbar, the lions of Rajasthan, lived far from Delhi in the shelter of their forests and hills. The vicinity of the Ranghars to the Mogul capital helps to explain their submission; it does not explain the relative virility and vitality of the breed to-day compared with their Hindu Rajput contemporaries. It will be generally admitted, I think, that the average Ranghar or Khaim Khani is a stouter man than the Rajput pure and simple. Why this should be so; why the descendants of the unconverted Rajputs who held by their faith should not produce as hard a breed of men as the Rajputs who were the first to submit to Islam, and that under compulsion, is a mystery unexplained. One does not set much store by converts in the East. They are generally a yielding, submissive crew. But the Ranghar is very decidedly "lord of himself," a man of action, with something of the pagan in him perhaps, but no hidden corners in his mind where sophistry can enter in and corrupt. The best answer I have heard to the Hun Jehadist wile was given by a Ranghar.

It was in the Shabkadr show on the 5th September, 1915, when the Mohmunds had the support of the Afghan Ningrahahis under the notorious Jan Badshah, who came in against us in defence of the Amir. There had been some hot scrapping. Our cavalry were clearing a village out Michni way in the afternoon, and had had heavy casualties in horses and men. The scene was a long, walled compound, from which we had been sniped at for hours. Into this rode half a dozen men of the 1st D.Y.O. Lancers, headed by the Ranghar Jemadar Rukkun-ud-din. The colonel of the regiment, standing up in his stirrups, saw the whole affair from over the wall, and heard the first parley, or rather the Afghans' impudent Jehadist appeal and the Ranghars' answer to it. As the Lancers cantered through the gate three abreast, the head of the Afghan crowd stepped forward, gave them the Muhammadan greeting, and with the confidence of an unassailable argument cried out to them, "We are of the true faith. Ye are of the true faith. Why then do ye fight for unbelieving Kafirs?" For answer Jemadar Rukkun-ud-din drew his revolver and shot the man in the stomach where he stood. In the scrimmage that followed the two parties were evenly matched in respect of numbers. No one gave quarter; in fact, no quarter had been given or taken all day; it is not the Mohmund or the Afghan habit, and they do not understand it. The sowars were mounted, and rode in with their lances; the Afghans were unmounted, but their magazines were full, and they fired a volley at the Lancers as they charged. Two sowars fell wounded, but not mortally. There was pandemonium in the compound for the next forty seconds, the Afghans running round and firing, the Ranghars galloping and swerving to get in their thrust. The lance beat the rifle every time, for the Afghan found the point and the menace of impact, and the plunging horse too unsteadying for accurate aim. In less than a minute they were all borne down.

Some one suggested that in the natural course of events Rukkun-ud-din would receive a reward, but the astute Colonel, said in the hearing of all—

"Reward! What talk is this of reward? What else could a Ranghar do but kill the man who insulted him. It would be a deep shame to have failed."

At the moment the speech was worth more than a decoration. It made the Ranghars feel very Ranghar-like—and that is the best thing that a Ranghar can feel, the best thing for himself and for his regiment. Incidentally the decoration came. One has not to search for pretexts for bestowing honour on men like these.

There was another youngster in that *melee* who deserved an I.O.M., a lance-duffadar, a lad of twenty. He had been hit in the seat from behind. The colonel heard of it and noticed that the lad was still mounted.

"You are wounded?" he asked.

"Sahib, it is nothing."

"Answer my question. Where were you hit?"

The boy for the first time showed signs of distress.

"Sahib," he said hesitatingly, "it is a shameful thing. These dogs were spitting in every corner. I have been wounded in the back."

He was made to dismount. His saddle was ripped by a bullet and sodden with blood.

"You must go back to the ambulance, young man," his Colonel told him.

"Sahib, I cannot go back in a doolie like a woman."

He was allowed to mount, though it was an extraordinarily nasty wound for the saddle. A weight seemed to be lifted from him when the Colonel explained that to a Ranghar and a cavalryman a wound in the back could only mean one was a good thruster and well in among the enemy when one was hit.

THE MEENA

I FOUND the Meenas of the Deoli regiment in a backwater of the Euphrates some days' journey from anywhere. They were so far from anywhere that when we came round a bend in the river in our bellam the sight of their white camp on the sand, and the gunboat beside it, made me feel that we had reached the coast after a voyage of inland exploration. The Meenas were a little tired of Samawa, where nothing happened. They wanted to be brigaded; they wanted to fight; they wanted at least to get up to Baghdad. They had to wait a long time before any of these desires were fulfilled. Nevertheless, although they had reasons to think themselves forgotten, they were a cheery crowd.

There are two classes of Meenas—those of the 42nd Deoli regiment, the Ujlas, Padhiars and Motis, who claim to have Rajput blood in them, and the purely aboriginal stock enlisted by

To face p. 188.] THE MEENA.

the 43rd Erinpura regiment from Sirohi and Jodhpur. I expected to find the Deoli Meenas small, alert, suspicious-looking men of the Bhīl, Santal, or Sawarah cast. I was surprised to discover them tall and stolid; pleasant, honest, plain in feature; and offering great variety in type. The Rajput blood is no myth. They do not look the least like aboriginals, and you could find the double of many of them among Dogras, Jats, Mahrattas, and Rajputana and Punjabi Mussalmans. This normal Aryan appearance is no doubt partly the impression of discipline, drill, confidence, training. In their own hills, before they enlisted they were a wild and startled-looking breed. And they had curious customs. One was that a man on losing his father had the right to sell his mother. In the days when they were first recruited you had to pay a man four annas to come in for a drill. The Meena would arrive with his bow and arrow, which were deposited in the quarter-guard. He was taught drill and paid for a day's work. He then picked up his bow and arrow and departed. Gradually, as they realised that no harm came of it, they began to settle and to bring their families into cantonments. But they were so distrustful of us in the beginning that we had to pay them every evening after the day's work.

The taming of the Meena and the genesis of the Deoli cantonment were slowly evolved processes. The history of it reads like an account of the domestication of a wild creature. First the Meena was encouraged to build. A collection of huts was soon grouped together, and the men lived in them. Each man built his own hut, and when he left the regiment sold it to his successor. After some little time they asked if they might bring their wives and families to live in them. This marked the beginning of an unalienable confidence, but the Meena was already imbued with a faith in his British officer. In after days, when the old huts were pulled down and regimental lines constructed, the men still lived in their own quarters, and this proprietary right was maintained until a few years ago. The motto of the regiment, "E turba legio," well describes the method of raising it.

Suspicion is the natural inheritance of the Meenas. They are the sons of cattle-lifters, dacoits, and thieves. For centuries they plundered the Rajput and were hunted down by him. It was the British who helped the Rajput to subdue them. To clear the district they infested it was necessary to cut down the jungle. The Meenas were gradually rounded up and confined to a prescribed area—the Meena Kerar, which lies partly in Jaipur and partly in Udaipur and Bundi, and is administered by the Political Agent at Deoli. Roll was called at night in the villages, and the absentee was the self-proclaimed thief. The system still holds in the more impenitent communities, but the restrictions on the Meena's movements are becoming fewer as he conforms with the social contract. The pleasing thing about it is that he bears us no grudge for the part we played in breaking him in. Like his neighbours, the Mer and the Merat, he recognises the British as the truest friends he has.

The simplicity, disingenuousness, and friendliness of the Meena are unmistakable. They are the most responsive people, and as sepoys, through contact with their British officers, they soon lose the habit of suspicion. I spent half a day with the Indian officers, and neither I nor they were bored. They like talking, and intersperse their conversation with ready and obvious jokes. It seemed to me that though they had

had most of the mischief knocked out of them, they retained a good deal of their superstition and childishness. That was to be expected, but one missed the shyness and sensitiveness that generally go with superstition. They were curiously frank and communicative about their odd beliefs. Like the old Thugs they have faith in omens. The Subadar showed me the lucky and unlucky fingers, and I gathered that if the jackal howls twice on the right, one's objective in a night march is as good as gained; if thrice on the left, the stars are unpropitious, and the enterprise should be abandoned. In November, 1914, the regiment was moved to Lahore to do railway defence work. The morning the battalion left the railway station where they entrained most of the men did puja (homage) to the engine, standing with open mouths, and fingers tapping foreheads. The railway is fifty-eight miles from cantonments in Deoli, and it was the first train that many of them had seen. Until the regiment moved opinions were divided as to whether the Meenas would continue to enlist. Such an upheaval and migration had not happened since the Afghan war. Wild rumours flew round the villages, but the Commanding Officer, by a wise system of letting a few men return on leave to their homes to spread the good news that the regiment was well and happy, soon quieted the countryside. Living so far out of the world they are naturally clannish. There is as much keenness about winning a hockey match against an outside team as there is in the final for a house-cup in an English public school. And here in Mesopotamia they were full of challenge. They wanted to show what Deoli could do, but as luck would have it there was not a Turk within a hundred and fifty miles.

The most delightful story I got out of the Subadar was the history of a Meena dynasty which ruled in Rajputana in the good old days before the gods became indifferent. I learnt that the proud Rajputs who claim descent from the sun and the moon are really interlopers who dispossessed the Meena by an act of treachery a hundred years ago.

"Fifteen princes have been Rajputs," the Subadar told me. "Before that the Meenas were kings. The last Meena king was the sixteenth from now."

"What was his name?" I asked.

"Sahib, I have forgotten his name—but he was childless. One day, when he was riding out, he met a Rajput woman who carried a child unborn. 'Your son shall be the child of my heart,' he told her; and when the boy was born he brought him up, and made him commander of his horse."

"Did he adopt him?"

"Sahib, he could not adopt him. The custom was in those days that when the old king died, the new king must be one of his line. Thus the gadi would pass to his brother's son, a Meena. No Rajput could inherit. Nevertheless, he treated the boy as his child. And then, Sahib, one day when the boy came back from seeing the Emperor at Delhi, he killed the king and all his relatives, and the whole army. It was like this, Sahib. It was the Kinaghat festival, when the king and all his people used to go down to the river without arms, and sprinkle water for the dead. It was the old custom, Sahib, and no one had ever made use of it for an evil purpose. But the Rajput secretly gathered his men behind a hill, and when the king and his people had cast aside their arms, and were performing the holy rite, the Rissaldar and other Rajputs fell upon them and killed them all, so that there was not a Meena left alive within a great distance of the place of slaughter. That is how the Rajput became the master, and the Meena his servant."

The Subadar's solemn "Again Huzoor" as he introduced each new phase in the tragedy was inimitable, but there was nothing tragic or resentful in his way of telling it. It was a tale comfortable to Meena pride, and therefore it was believed as legends are believed all over the world which make life easier and give one a stiffer back or a more honourable ancestry.

The Subadar told me that the books of the Meena bards had been confiscated. They are locked up in the fort at Ranatbawar, and no one may enter. If any one reads them, the Rajput dynasty will pass away, and the Meena will be restored; therefore the Rajputs would like to destroy them, but there is some ancient inhibition. The chronicles are put away in an iron chest under the ground; yet, as the Subadar explained, the record is indestructible. It has lived in men's memories and hearts, new epics have been written, and the story is handed down from father to son. Another Meena told me the story is written "in the Political Agent's Book at Jaipur." This, I think, was by way of reference rather than confirmation, for it could never have entered any of their heads that one could doubt the genuineness or authenticity of the tale. When the usurper was crowned a Meena was called in from afar to put the tilak, or caste mark, on the king's forehead. And here the fairy story comes in again, for the tilak was imprinted on the king's brow by the Meena's toe. This is still the custom, the Subadar assured me, and he explained that it was a humiliation imposed upon the king by the priests as an atonement for his bad faith. The priest persuaded the king that the only way that he could hope to keep his throne was by receiving the tilak from the toe of the Meena, and he appeased his vanity by pretending that the Meena, by raising his toe, signified submission, just as the Yankee talks about turning up his toe to the daisies.

Here the Subadar was becoming too subtle for me, and I felt that I was getting out of my depth. But there was another point which was quite clear and simple. It bore out his theory of an hereditary obligation which the Rajput owes the Meena by way of restitution. In Jaipur and Alwar the Ujla Meenas are the custodians of the State treasure. I used to think that they were appointed on the same principle as the Chaukidar who would be a thief if he were not a guardian of the property under his trust. But in this I wronged the Meena. The Ujlas are honourable office-holders. When the Maharaja of Jaipur comes to the gadi he has to take an oath that he will not diminish his inheritance, and he is responsible to the Ujlas that anything that he may take away in times of famine or other emergency shall be restored. The old Subadar took this as a matter of pride. He was quite content with his ancestry—if indeed he bothered his head about the status of the Meena at all. The legend of the regicide rissaldar was well found. You could tell by the way he told the story that he was pleased with it. One hears yarns of the kind, comforting tales of legendary wrong, all over the world, in Hottentot wigwams and Bloomsbury lodging-houses. The difference is only in degree. They contribute mildly to self-respect; the humble are rehabilitated in garments of pride; and very few of those who inherit the myth look for the miracle of reversion.

The Meenas are as contented a people as you could find, a cheery, simple, frugal, hardy race. The old Subadar boasted that his men never fell out. "Even when the mules fall out," he told me, "they go on." They are very brave in the jungle, and will stand up to a wounded leopard or tiger. The Meena is a good shot, and a fine shikari. He will find his way anywhere in the dark, and he never loses himself. He ought to be useful in a night raid. He is a trifle hot-headed, I gathered. In the divisional manœuvres near Nasiriyeh the cavalry were coming down on a line of them in open country, when they fixed bayonets and charged. "They are a perfectly splendid crowd," one of the officers told me, "I should dearly love to see them go into action, and take twenty-five per cent. casualties. It would be the making of them." But his Meenas had no luck. No doubt, if they had been given a chance, they would have fought as well as the best. It was their misfortune that they came too late, and that they were sent up the wrong river. In the meanwhile, at Deoli, recruits are pouring in.

Every village contains a number of old pensioners who, like my friend the Subadar, love to talk of their own deeds, the prowess of their Sahibs, and how they marched with the regiment towards Kabul. The young men stand round and listen, and are fired with emulation, and there is no doubt that if the Sircar wants them the contingent of Meenas will increase. They are not a very numerous class, but they are steadfast and loyal. The love of honour and adventure will spread as wide a net among them as conscription, and there will be no jiwans seen in the villages who are not home on leave.

THE JHARWAS

(BY AN OFFICER WHO HAS COMMANDED THEM)

THERE are not many aboriginals in the Indian Army—a few Brahuis from the borders of Beluchistan, the Mers and Merats and Meenas from the hills and jungles of Rajputana, and the Jharwas of Assam. The word "Jharwa" is the Assamese term for a "jungle-man," and how it came to be generally applied to the enlisted man from Assam and Cachar is lost in the obscurity of years. It is now the usual term for any sepoy who hails from these parts, with the exception of the Manipuri.

When the Sylhet local battalion, afterwards the 44th Sylhet Light Infantry, now the 1/8th Gurkha Rifles, was raised on February 19th, 1824, it was composed of Sylhetis, Manipuris, and the surrounding tribes of Cachar, which province took its name from the Cacharis, who settled there at the beginning of the seventeenth century, having been driven out of the Assam

To face p. 200.] THE JHARWA.

valley by the Ahoms, or Assamese, and Muhammadans. The plainsmen of Assam were very warlike till the Muhammadan invasion in the sixteenth century, when they were so thoroughly overcome they fell an easy prey to the Burmese, who were finally driven out of Assam and Cachar by the British in 1824–26, since when the Assamese have settled down peacefully.

The principal races, now enlisted under the name of Jharwa, are the Mech, the Kachari, and the Rawa. The Mech mostly came from the region of Jalpaiguri, and spread eastwards. The Kachari were the original inhabitants of Assam; they are also found in Cachar, and are of the Koch stock, from whom Coochbehar takes its name; they generally call themselves Rajbansi, "of princely race." The Rawa (Ahoms) are also original Assamese. There are, besides, the Garos, who come from the Goalpara district. All the three former are Hindu converts, and show much more caste prejudice than the Gurkha does, though he, in turn, is not impressed with their Hindu claims. He raises no objection, however, to living under the same barrack-roof with them, but will not eat their food. In the old days, the Jharwa proved his value as a soldier in all the fighting in the valleys of Assam and Cachar, and surrounding hills. He rid the low country of the Khasias, who were the terror of the plains, as can be seen from the "The Lives of the Lindsays" and a recent publication "The Records of Old Sylhet," compiled by Archdeacon Firminger. The first troops engaged in the subjugation of the Khasias and Jaintias in their hills were Jharwas of the Sylhet battalion; the campaign began in 1829, and was continued at intervals until 1863, when the Jaintia rebellion was finally stamped out. Two companies of Gurkhas were brought into this regiment in 1832, and by degrees the Jharwa ceased to be enlisted in the regular army, till at last, in 1891, it was ordered that no more were to be taken. This was the time of the Magar and Gurung boom; in fact, except as regards the Khas, it was not considered the thing to enlist any other Gurkha races in the army. The fact that the Gurkha regiments up country earned their name with a large admixture of Garhwalis in their ranks, in the same way as the Assam regiments earned theirs with the help of many Jharwas, seemed largely to be lost sight of, and though the Jharwa had continued to do yeoman service in the ranks of the Assam Military Police, it was not till 1915 that it was thought worth while to try him in the regular army again. After the war, a regular Jharwa Regiment raised and stationed in Assam should be a most efficient unit, and a most valuable asset on that somewhat peculiar frontier.

The Jharwa is a curious creature in many ways. He has nothing in common with the Gurkha, except his religion, and to a certain extent his appearance; nor is he even a hillman. Till he joins, he has probably never done a hard day's work, nor any regular work, but has earned his living by cutting timber, or doing a little farming in a rich and fertile country where a man does not need to do much to keep himself. He is more intelligent than the Gurkha, and has, as a rule, a fairly good ear for music; he is lazy, hard to train, and not very clean in his person, unless well looked after, but he is a first-class man at any jungle work. The last of the old lot of Jharwas in the 1/8th Gurkhas, Havildar Madho Ram (Garoo), won the Macgregor Memorial medal, in 1905, for exploration and survey work in Bhutan. Others again are intensely stupid. In October 1916, a Military Police havildar came out in charge of a small draft to Mesopotamia, and his C.O. tried to find out how much he knew about practical soldiering. He put him in charge of a squad of men, and told him to exercise them. The worthy havildar was soon in a fix. When asked how he rose to be havildar, he replied that he was promoted because he was a good wood-cutter and repairer of buildings. The C.O. asked him where he was to get wood to cut in Mesopotamia, upon which he looked round vacantly on all sides and remarked, "Jhar na hoi" ("there is no jungle"), whereupon he was sent back to look after the regimental dump. Where the Jharwa fails is as an officer or non-commissioned officer, since for generations he has never been in a position to enforce or give implicit and prompt obedience. In Assam, it is all one to the ordinary villager whether he does a thing now or next week; a high standard of work or punctuality has never been expected of him, consequently he does not expect it of anyone else, and a good many N.C.O.'s got the surprise of their life when they found that the excuse, "I told them, but they didn't do it," would not go down. But in jungle work there are few to touch him, and he has proved his grit in the stress of modern battle. Many years ago, I was following up a wounded buffalo in the Nambhar forest, and one of our men was walking in front of me, snicking the creepers and branches, which stretched across the track, with a little knife as sharp as a razor. Suddenly, without a word, he sprang to one side to clear my front, and there lay the huge beast about ten yards off, luckily stone dead. It requires some nerve to walk up to a wounded buffalo, without any sort of weapon to defend oneself with. In the winter of 1916–17, a small party of the 7th Gurkhas swam the Tigris, to reconnoitre the Turk position near Chahela. They carried out their work successfully, but two Jharwas, who had volunteered to go with the party, were overcome with the cold, and were drowned coming back. The surviving Gurkhas all got the I.O.M. or D.S.M. On February 17th, 1917, at Sannaiyat, a signaller, attached to the 1/8th Gurkhas, Lataram Mech, took across his telephone wire into the second Turkish line under very heavy shell-fire, which wiped out the N.C.O. and another of his party of four, established communication with battalion headquarters and the line behind him, and, when that part of the trench was recaptured, came back across the open and rolled up his wire, under fire all the time. On the same day another Jharwa lad, when he got into the Turkish trench, flung away his rifle and belt, and ran amok with his kukri. He broke that one and came back, covered with blogd from head to foot, into our front trench to get another, when he went forward again. I could never find out his name. If he was not killed, he lay low, probably thinking he would be punished for losing his rifle.

At Istabulat, another Jharwa (Holiram Garo) got separated from the rest of his party, and attacked a part of the Turk position by himself. Although wounded in the head, he lay on the front of the enemy's parapet, and sniped away till dark, when he returned to his platoon, and asked for more ammunition. For this he got the I.O.M. The poor little Jharwa did wonderfully well, seeing that, till he left Assam, his horizon had been bounded by the Bhootan-Tibet range on one side and the Patkoi on the other. He had never seen guns, cavalry, trenches, or anything to do with real warfare. Although reared in the damp enervating climate of the plains of Assam, he stuck the intense cold and heat, as well as food to which he had never been accustomed, without grumbling, whilst the doctors said his endurance of pain in hospital was every bit as good as the Gurkha's, and an example to all the other patients. Till 1915, the authorities knew nothing about him, his antecedents, or peculiarities, so he was looked on as merely an untidy sort of Gurkha, with whom, as said before, he had no affinity, besides not having anything like the same physical strength.

Before we went out to Mesopotamia, my regiment was detailed to counter an expected raid on a certain part of the Indian coast. We entrained at midnight, and in the morning it was reported we had fifty more men than we started with. It turned out that a party of fifty Jharwas had arrived at the railway station, just before we left, and when they realised that the regiment was going off without them, they made a rush, crowded in where they could, and came along, leaving all their kit on the platform. This, if not exactly proving good discipline, showed at any rate they were not lacking in keenness and enterprise.

THE DRABI

In the Great War the Drabi has come by his own. He is now a recognised combatant. At Shaiba and Sahil alone six members of the transport corps were awarded the Indian Order of Merit. This is as it should be, for before August, 1914, there was only one instance recorded of a Drabi receiving a decoration.

The Drabi is recruited from diverse classes, but he is generally a Punjabi Mussalman, not as a rule of the highest social grade, though he is almost invariably a very worthy person. If I were asked to name the agents to whom we owe the maintenance of our empire in the East, I should mention, very high in the list, the Drabi and the mule. No other man, no other beast, could adequately replace them. There are combinations of the elements which defeat the last word of scientific transport. And that is where the Drabi, with his pack mules or A.T. carts, comes in.

In France, when the motor-lorries were stuck in the mud, we thanked God for the mule and the Drabi. I remember my delight one day when I saw a convoy of Indian A.T. carts swinging down the road, the mules leaning against one another as pack mules will do when trained to the yoke. The little convoy pulled up outside the courtyard of an abattoir in an old town in Picardy, where it had been raining in torrents for days, until earth and water had produced a third element which resembled neither. The red-peaked kula protruding from the khaki turban of the Drabi proclaimed a Punjabi Mussalman. Little else was distinguishable in the mist and rain, which enveloped everything in a dismal pall. The inert bundle of misery unrolled itself and, seeing a Sahib by the gate, saluted.

"Bad climate," I suggested.

"Yes, Sahib, very bad climate."

"Bad country?"

But the man's instinctive sense of conciliation was proof against dampness, moral or physical.

"No, Sahib. The Sircar's country is everywhere very good." The glint of a smile crept over the dull white of his eyes.

To the Drabi there are only two kinds of white people—the Sircar, or British Raj, and the enemy. The enemy is known to him only by the ponderous and erratic nature of his missiles, for the mule-cart corps belongs to the first line of transport.

"Where is your home?" I asked.

"Amritsar, Sahib."

I wondered whether he were inwardly comparing the two countries. Here, everything drenched and colourless; there, brightness and colour and clean shadows. Here, the little stone church of a similar drabness to its envelope of mist; there, the reflection of the Golden Temple sleeping in the tank all day. The minarets of his mosque and the crenellated city walls would be etched now against a blue sky. I looked at his mules. They did not seem at all *dépaysés*.

"How do they stand the damp?" I asked. "Much sickness?"

"No, Sahib. Only one has been sick. None have died except those destroyed by the bo-ombs."

I wondered what the carts were doing at ——. They were of the first line; the first line transport carries the food into the very mouth of the Army. Being the last link in the line of communications, it is naturally the most vulnerable. Other links are out of range of the enemy's guns and immune, in this phase of the operations at least, from attack except by aircraft. The Drabi explained that they had been detailed for forage work.

As he lifted the curricle bar from the yoke one of the mules stepped on his foot, and he called it a name that reflected equally on his own morals and those of the animal's near relations. He did not address the beast in the tone an Englishman would use, but spoke to it with brotherly reproach. Just then an officer of the Indian Army Supply and Transport Corps rode up, and I got him to talk, as I knew I could if I praised his mules and carts enough. He enlarged on the virtues of the most adaptable, adjustable, and indestructible vehicles that had ever been used in a campaign, and of the most hardy, ascetic, and providentially accommodating beast that had ever drawn or carried the munitions of war. These light transport-carts are wonderful. They cut through the mud like a harrow over thin soil. The centre of the road is left to the lorries. "They would be bogged where we go," the S. and T. man said proudly. "They are built for swamps and boulder-strewn mountain streams. If the whole show turns over, you can right it at once. If you get stuck in a shell-hole, you can cut the mules loose, use them as pack transport, and man-handle the carts. Then we have got component parts. We can stick on a wheel in a minute, and we don't get left like that menagerie of drays, furnishing vans, brewers' carts, and farmers' tumbrils, which collapse in the fairway and seem to have no extra parts at all—unadaptable things, some of them, like a lot of rotten curios. And, of course, you know you can take our carts to pieces and pack them; you can get"—I think he said fourteen—"of them into a truck. And if you——"

Then he enlarged on his beasts. Nothing ever hurts a mule short of a bullet or shell. Physical impact, heat or cold, or drought, or damp, it is all the same. They are a little fastidious about drink, but they deserve one indulgence, and a wise Staff officer will give them a place up-stream for watering above the cavalry. For hardiness nothing can touch them.

They are as fit in Tibet as in the Sudan, as composed in a blizzard on the Nathu-la as in a sandstorm at Wadi Halfa. And I knew that every word he said was true. I had sat a transport-cart through the torrents of Jammu, and had lost a mule over a precipice in a mountain pass beyond the Himalayas. It lay half buried in the snow all night with the thermometer below zero. In the morning it was dragged up by ropes and began complacently grazing.

"And look at them now in this slush!" They certainly showed no sign of distress or even of depression.

"And the Drabis? Do they grouse?"

"Not a bit. They are splendid. They have no nerves, no more nerves than the mules. You ought to have seen Muhammad Alim come back from Neuve Chapelle. When hell began the order had gone round 'All into your dug-outs,' and the bombardier of his cart had buried himself obediently in the nearest funkhole. He stuck it out there all day. The next morning he rolled up at the Brigade Column and reported his cart was lost. Nothing could have lived in that fire, so it was struck off."

But Drabi Muhammad Alim had not heard

the order. He sat through the whole of the bombardment in his cart. After two days, not having found his destination, he returned. "Sahib," he said, "I have lost the way." When asked what the fire was like he said that there had been a wind when the boom-golies passed, which reminded him of the monsoon when the tufân catches the pine trees in Dagshai.

It occurred to me that the Asiatic driver assimilated the peculiar virtues of his beast. The man with a camel or bullock or mule is less excitable, more of a fatalist, than the man who goes on foot alone. The mule and the Drabi would rattle along under shell-fire as imperturbably as they run the gauntlet of falling rocks on the Kashmir road in the monsoon. I have seen the Drabi calmly charioteering his pontoons to the Tigris bank, perched on a thwart like a bird, when the bullets were flying and the sappers preparing the bridge for the crossing. And I have seen him carry on when dead to the world, a mere automaton like Ali Hussein, who reported himself hit in the shoulder two days after the battle at Umm-el-Hannah. "Yes, Sahib," he admitted to the doctor a little guiltily when cross-examined, "it was in the battle two days ago that I came by this wound." Then he added shamefacedly fearing reproof, "Sahib, I could not come before. There was no time. There were too many journeys. And the wounded were too many."

When his neighbour is hit by his side, the Drabi buries himself more deeply into his wrappings. He does not want to pick up a rifle and kill somebody for shooting his "pale" as a Tommy would, but says, "My brother is dead. I too shall soon die." And he simply goes on prepared for the end, neither depressed at its imminence, nor unduly exalted if it be postponed. He is a worthy associate of those wonderful carts and mules.

In the evening I passed the abattoir again and looked over the gate. Inside there was a batch of camp followers who had come in from fatigue duty. I saw the men huddling over their fires in groups in that humped attitude of contented discomfort which only the Indian can assume. Their families in the far villages of the Punjab and the United Provinces would be squatting by their braziers in just the same way at this hour. Perhaps the Drabi would be thinking of them—if thought stirred within his brain—and of the golden slant light of the sun on the shisham and the orange siris pods and the pungent incense that rises in the evening from the dried cow-dung fire, a product, alas! which France with all its resources, so rich, varied, and inexhaustible, cannot provide.

THE SANTAL LABOUR CORPS

THE Labour Corps in Mesopotamia introduced the nearest thing to Babel since the original confusion of tongues. Coolies and artisans came in from China and Egypt, and from the East and West Indies, the aboriginal Santals and Paharias from Bengal, Moplahs, Thyas and Nayars from the West Coast, Nepalese quarrymen, Indians of all races and creeds, as well as the Arabs and Chaldeans of the country. They made roads and bunds, built houses, loaded and unloaded steamers and trucks, supplied carpenters, smiths and masons, followed the fighting man and improved the communications behind him, and made the land habitable which he had won.

One day I ran into a crowd of Santals on the Bridge of Boats in Baghdad. It was probably the first time that Babylon had drawn into its vortex the aboriginals of the hill tracts of Bengal. They were scurrying like a flock of sheep, not because they were rushed, I was told, but simply for fun. Some one had started it, and the others had broken into a jog-trot. One of them, with bricks balanced on his head, was playing a small reed flute—the Pipe of Pan. Another had stuck a spray of salmon-pink oleander in his hair. The full, round cheeks of the little men made their black skin look as if it had been sewn up tightly and tucked under the chin. They were like happy, black, golly-wogs, and the dust in their elfin locks, the colour of tow, increased the impish suggestion of the toy-shop. The expression on their faces is singularly happy and innocent, and endorses everything Rousseau said about primitive content. Evolution has spared them; they have even escaped the unkindness of war.

When the Santal left his home, all he took with him was two brass cooking-pots, his stick, and a bottle of mustard oil. The stick he uses to sling his belongings over his shoulder, with a net attached, and generally his boots inside. He loves to rub himself all over with oil, but in this unfruitful land he can find little or none, and he had not even time to refill at Bombay. On board ship he saw coal for the first time. Each man was given a brickette with his rations, for fuel, and Jangal, Baski, Goomda Kisku, and others put their vessel on the strange, black substance, and expected it to boil. A very simple, happy, and contented person is the Santal. Once gain his confidence, and he will work for you all day and half the night; abuse it, and he will not work at all.

I found them in their camp afterwards in a palm grove by the Tigris, not unlike a camp in their own land, only the palms were dates and not cocoanuts. Here the Santals were very much at home. The pensioned Indian officer in charge, a magnificent veteran, of the 34th Sikh Pioneers, with snowy beard and moustache and two rows of ribbons on his breast, was pacing up and down among these little dark men like a Colossus or a benevolent god. The old Subadar was loud in their praises. He had been on the staff of a convict Labour Corps, and so spoke from his heart.

"There is no fighting, quarrelling, thieving, lying among them, Sahib. If you leave anything on the ground, they won't pick it up. No trouble with women folk. No gambling. No tricks of deceit."

A British officer of the company who knew them in their own country told me the same tale.

"They are the straightest people I have ever struck," he said. "We raised nearly 1700 of them in the district, paid them a month's wages in advance, and told them to find their way to the nearest railway station, a journey of two or three days. They all turned up but one, and the others told us he had probably hanged himself because his wife would not let him go. They are very honest, law-abiding folk. They leave their money lying about in their tents, and it is quite safe. They have no police in their villages; the headman settles all their troubles. And there is no humbug about them. Other coolies slack off if you don't watch them, and put on a tremendous spurt when they see an officer coming along, and keep it up till he is out of sight. But the dear old Santal is much too simple for this. If the Army Commander came to see them they'd throw down their picks and shovels and stare at him till he went away. They are not thrusters; they go their own pace, but they do their day's work all right. And they are extraordinarily patient and willing. They'll work over time if you don't tell them to stop; and they'll turn out, if you ask them, and do an extra turn at a pinch, without grumbling, even if they have only just got back to camp and haven't had time to cook their food."

All this sounded very Utopian, but the glimpse of them on the Bridge of Boats, and an hour spent in their camp on Sunday morning, gave one the impression of children who had not been spoilt. We went the round of their tents, and they played to us on their flutes, the same pastoral strains one hears in villages all over the East; and they showed us the sika mark burnt in their forearms, always an odd number, which, like Charon's Obol, is supposed to give them a good send-off in the next world. They burn themselves, too, when they have aches and pains. One man had a scar on his forehead a week old, where he had applied a brand as a cure for headache. Nearly every Santal is a musician, and plays the drum or pipe. The skins of the drums had cracked in the heat at Makina, and they had left them behind, but they make flutes out of any material they can pick up. One of them blew off two of his fingers boring stops in the brass tube of a Turkish shell which had a fuse and an unexploded charge left in it. That is the only casualty among the Santals remotely connected with arms. It is an understood thing that they should not go near the firing line. Once an aeroplane bomb fell near the corps. They looked up like a frightened herd. A second came sizzling down within a hundred yards of them, and they took to their heels. A little man showed me how he had run, rehearsing a pantomime of panic fright, with his bandy legs, and doubled fist pummelling the air.

The Santals came out on a one year's agreement, as they must get back to their harvest. But they will sign on again. They have no quarrel with Mesopotamia. Twenty rupees a month, and everything found, is a wage that a few years ago would have seemed beyond the dreams of avarice. They are putting on weight; fare better than they have ever done, and their families are growing rich. Most of them have their wages paid in family allotments at home, generally to their elder brother, father, or son, rather than their wife. The Santals are distrustful of women as a sex. "What if I were labouring here," one of them said, "and she were to run off with another man and the money?"

The women are not permitted to attend the sacrifices in the Holy Grove, or to eat the flesh of offerings, or to climb the consecrated trees, or to know the name of the family's secret god lest they should betray it; or even, save in the case of a wife or unmarried daughter, to enter the chamber where the household god dwells in silent communion with the ancestors. Save for these restrictions the relations between men and women in the tribe are happy and free. In social life the women are very independent and often masters in the house. They are a finer physical type, and the men of the tribe are proud to admit it. The corps was collecting firewood when one of the officers twitted a man on the meagre size of his bundle.

"Look at the Arabs," he said. "Even the women carry a bigger load than you."

But the Santal was not abashed. He did not resent this reflection upon himself; it was the carrying power of his own women he defended. "Our women, too, carry much bigger loads than we do," he said ingenuously.

There is a curious reticence about names among the Santals. Husband and wife will not mention each other's names, not even when speaking of some one else bearing the same name. When receiving her allotment from a British officer the Santal woman has to call in a third person to name the absent husband. It would be a species of blasphemy to divulge the secret herself. There is a table of degrees of relationship in which the mention of names is taboo among the tribes, similar to the catalogue prohibiting intermarriage of kin in our Prayer Book. And, of course, it is quite useless to ask a Santal his age. Dates and sums of money are remembered by the knots tied in a string; but the birth date is not accounted of any importance. "How old are you?" the O. C. of the corps asked one of these bearded men of the woods. "Sahib," the Santal replied, after some puckering of the brow in calculation, "I am at least five years old."

There is one comfort the Santal misses when away from home. He must have his handi, or rice beer, or if not his handi, at least some substitute that warms his inside. They said they would make their own handi in Mesopotamia if we gave them the rice; but they discovered it could not be done. Either they had not the full ingredients, or their women had the secret of the brew. Hence the order for a tri-weekly issue of rum. Many of the Santals were once debarred from becoming Christians, fearing that the new faith meant abstention from the tribal drink.

This summer the Santals will be at home again, drinking their handi, looking after their crops and herds, reaping the same harvest, thinking the same thoughts, playing the same plaintive melodies on their pipes, as when Nebuchadnezzar ruled in Babylon. Three dynasties of Babylon, Assyria, Chaldea, and the Empire of the Chosroes, have risen and crumbled away on the soil where he is labouring now, and all the while the Santal has led the simple life, never straying far from the Golden Age, never caught up in the unhappy train of Progress. And so his peace is undisturbed by the seismic convulsions of Armageddon; he has escaped the crown that *Kultur* has evolved at Karlsruhe and Essen and Potsdam. At harvest-time, while the Aryan is still doing military duties, the Santal will be reaping in the fields. As soon as the crops are in, there is the blessing of the cattle, then five days and nights of junketing, drinking and dancing, bathing and sacrifice, shooting at a target with the bow, and all the licence of high festival. Then after a month or two he will return to the fringe of the Great War, and bring with him his friends. He will fall to again, and take up his pick and shovel, the most contented man in Iraq.

THE INDIAN FOLLOWER

THE Drabi and Kahar[1] are no longer followers. They are combatants and eligible for decorations, and their names appear in the columns of honour in the Army List, and occupy an increasing space. If cooks, syces, bhisties, bearers and sweepers were eligible too, their names would also appear; for the war has proved that chivalry exists under the most unlikely exteriors. A great deal has been written about the Drabi and the Kahar, and their indifference to danger. The nature of their work keeps them constantly under fire, whether they are bringing up rations to the trenches, or searching the ground for the wounded. The recognition of them as combatants is a belated act of justice, and one wishes that the devotion of the humbler menial classes could be recognised in the same way. One meets followers of the wrong kind, but the old type of Indian servant has increased his prestige

[1] Stretcher-bearer.

in the war. Officers who did not know him before are impressed with his worth. He has shown courage in emergency, and, what is more, he has the British habit, only in the passive voice, of "slogging on."

One admires the Indian's impassivity under fire, and one is sometimes led into neglecting cover on account of it. It does not do for the Sahib to sneak along behind an A.T. cart when the Drabi is taking his chance with the mules in front. In France I heard an amusing story of a Sergeant-Major who had to thread a bombarded area much more slowly than his wont, on account of the sang-froid of a syce. An officer was taking an extra horse with him into Ypres at a time when the town was beginning to establish its reputation for unpleasantness, and he came in for a heavy bombardment. Besides the usual smaller stuff, seventeen-inch shells were coming over like rumbling trains, and exploding with a burst like nothing on earth. The officer wished he had left his second horse behind, and was wondering if it would be safe to send his syce back on the chance of his finding the new dump when he met the Sergeant-Major who was returning direct to it. The Sergeant-Major undertook to show the syce the way, and to look after him. When next the two met, the officer asked the Sergeant-Major if the syce had given him any trouble.

"Trouble, sir! He came along fast enough until we got to the *pavé*. Then he pulled up, and wouldn't go out of a walk. It was as nasty a mess-up as ever I've been in, but he wouldn't quit his walk."

The Sergeant-Major's language, I believe, was as explosive as his surroundings; but the syce humbly repeated that it was the Sahib's orders never to go out of a walk where there was hard ground or stones, and "here it was all stones." Five battery mules were knocked out, and a syce and horse killed next door to him; stilled he walked—or capered, for the horse, even more than the sergeant-major, was for taking over charge.

I remember an old cook of the Black Watch who persisted in wearing a saucepan on his head in the trenches at Sannaiyat when the Turks were bombarding us. The man had to be humoured, so a special cooking vessel—rather a leaky one—was set aside by the mess-sergeant for his armoury. He was nervous because the regimental bhistie had been killed by a shell. There was great lamentation in the battalion when the bhistie fell. The bhistie, that silent, willing drudge, is always a favourite with the British soldier. His gentleness, patience, and devotion are proverbial. Even in cantonments, bent under the weight of his massaq,[1] he is invested with a peculiar dignity, and in desert places he appears as one of the few beneficent manifestations of Providence. One always thinks of him as a giver; his bestowals are without number, his demands infinitesimal. I have never heard of a grumbling, or impatient, or morose bhistie, or of one whose name has been associated actively or passively with violence, or provocation, or crime. There was a dreadful day during the Ahwaz operations in May, 1915, when our troops, after a stifling night, found the wells they had counted on were dry. They were already exhausted; the temperature was 125 degrees in the shade, or would have been if there had been any shade, and to reach water they had another ten or fifteen miles' march to Kharkeh. An officer in the Indian Cavalry told me that he watched a

[1] Waterskin.

To face p. 230.] BHIL FOLLOWERS

bhistie of the Merwara battalion supporting a man, who was too weak to walk unaided, for more than two miles. When the sepoy came to the end of his tether the bhistie stayed with him a few seconds, and then relieved him of his rifle which he carried into camp. That was probably the hottest and thirstiest day's march our troops endured in Mesopotamia. A number of the Merwaras died of thirst. It was just before Dunlop's burning march over the desert by Illah and Bisaitin to Amara, when even the most hard-bitten old campaigners fell through heat-exhaustion. During all these operations the bhisties behaved splendidly at a time when any form of effort was a virtue, fetching water untiringly and pouring it over the victims of the march.

The bearer, too, has played up well when he has had the chance. During the retirement from Ctesiphon the last batch of boats to leave Kut just before the siege came in for a good deal of sniping. One of them put ashore at a bend, and landed a party which took up a position on the bank and tried to keep down the enemy's fire. This was very early in the morning. "It was quite a hot corner," an officer told me. "I had spotted a man who had crawled up to within a hundred and fifty yards of us, and was drawing a bead on him. I had clean forgotten the boat, and Kut, and the retreat, and all the rest of it, when I heard a familiar voice behind me, 'Tea ready, sorr.' It was good old Dubru, my Madrasi bearer, who had come up under fire. The tea was good and the buttered toast still hot. His only remark when I had finished it was 'Master like another cup?' I should have been very unhappy if the old fellow had been hit."

I could multiply instances of the providence that keeps the follower to his prescribed task, whether in emergency or in the ordinary day's work. A medical officer was going round his camp during a bombardment, to see that his staff were taking cover. He found the infection ward in a great state of perturbation—not from fright as might have been expected. The trouble was a violation of the rules. "Sir," a Babu explained to him, "it is a serious matter, no doubt, two contact cases have escaped confinement of ward." It was his way of saying that two men with mumps had had the sense to discover a funk-hole and make themselves scarce.

The name of the sweeper is associated with chivalry in an ironic sense only. His Indian titles "Mehtar" and "Jemadar" are facetiously honorific, as when one speaks of him as "the knight." Yet the sweeper has won laurels in the war. It was at Givenchy, I think, at the very beginning of things, when cartridges were jammed in the magazines, and men were wanted to take ramrods to the front, and there were no spare combatants for errands of this kind, that the sweepers carried the ramrods over the open ground with no cover of communication trenches to the men in the firing line. In Mesopotamia a sweeper of the —th Rifles took an unauthorised part in an assault on the Turkish lines, picked up the rifle of a dead sepoy, and went on firing until he was shot in the head.

What are the elements of the follower's sang-froid? In the case of this sweeper it can only have been the love of honour or adventure, but he was a very exceptional man, and one cannot expect to find the same spirit in the normal drudge. The good old Drabi who, when the bullets are flicking round, pulls his blanket about his ears and subsides a little in his cart is not of this mould. In an analysis of the composition of his courage lack of imagination would play a part, and fatalism, which becomes a virtue in the presence of death; but the main thing, and this explains two-thirds of his stiffening, is that it never enters his head that it is possible not to carry on with his job. In the follower's honest, slow brain, the processes which complicate decision in subtler minds are clotted into one—the sense of order, continuity, routine, everything that is implied in a regulation. These things are of the laws of necessity. He does not know it, but "carrying on" is his gospel, philosophy, and creed.

Published by

Facsimile Publisher
Ashok Vihar, Delhi-110052 (India)
Website: www.facsimilepublisher.com

Distributed by

Gyan Books Pvt. Ltd.
5, Ansari Road, Daryaganj, New Delhi-110002 (India)
E-mail: books@gyanbooks.com, Website: www.gyanbooks.com